The Last Green Beret

The Last Green Beret

By

Robert J. Kelly

ISBN1-58721-248-X

1st Books-rev. 4/25/00

About The Book

'The Last Green Beret' is a fast-paced espionage story that takes place in modern day America. The main character, Roger, is a retired Green Beret and CIA operative who is drawn back into the world of clandestine operations when his daughter is kidnaped by terrorists. The story takes many turns during Roger's quest to rescue his daughter, and he uncovers the truth behind a myriad of 20th century political events during his mission, including Watergate and the Kennedy assassination. The reader is taken for an emotional roller coaster ride when he realizes the superficial plot is not the obvious.

Other novels by Robert J. Kelly:

Gift's of the Gods
A Cop's Cop

This book is a work of fiction. Names, characters and events are either products of the author's imagination or are used fictitiously. Any resemblance to actual people, living or dead, or events, is entirely coincidental.

Woof

1

The kisses to the nape of her neck never grew tiresome. She had been with many men during her 43 years, but did not find satisfaction until she met him. The rhythm of their bodies grinding in perfect harmony increased until she was overcome by a high of mountainistic freedom. She let out a moan and then a groan that turned into a cry. He released his physical love deep inside her and kissed her neck while whispering sweet nothings in her ear. One of their trysts, five years prior, produced a beautiful child. Patricia, or Tris as her parents called her, had dusty brown hair, green eyes and was full of piss and vinegar.

Catherine Polk Brown, Cathy to her friends in Austin and Cat to her husband (a small compromise she was glad to make), dropped out of high school to join a commune with her hippie lover at age 17. Unfortunately, it was 1972 and the beginning of the end of the hippie- peace-love era. She followed the commune to northern California and was left stranded when her lover took a fancy to another girl in the group. Cathy made her way back from California, but it took four years, countless jobs as a waitress and several bouts of prostitution to help pay for two abortions. When she finally arrived in her home town of Austin, Texas she was heartbroken to learn her mom had lost a battle to ovarian cancer and passed away four months prior to her return. Cathy had no siblings, her only living relative was her father; who had remarried a woman 15 years his junior. Her father and his young bride were expecting their first child, and he had no intentions of disrupting their new life. He gave Cathy $500.00 and the name of a friend in the personnel department of a meat packing plant. He made it quite clear she was never to contact him again. Cathy took the money and said goodbye, seeing the only bridge to her past crumble behind her as she left.

The next 16 years was a journey down the river Styx. With no formal education, Cathy was always the first to go when there was a lay-off. To her credit, she stayed mentally tough and earned her GED when she was 32. She worked two part-time jobs, one as a cleaning woman and one as a bookkeeper at a small printing firm. The bookkeeper position almost branded her with the scarlet letter for an affair she had with her boss. Cathy's other relationships were either abusive or founded on drugs and alcohol. When she turned 35 she decided she had had enough and entered a thirty-day treatment program at a local clinic. Clean and sober for the first time in her adult life, Cathy rented a room in a small boarding house 40 miles west of Austin. The landlord required money up front and Cathy was only able to guarantee a two week stay. Her luck changed the first day she looked for a job and she was offered a position as a waitress at a local diner. The work was hard and the tips only fair, but Cathy had a new start in life. She cut her blond hair short, used very little make-up, and wore her uniform a size too large in an effort to hide her attractive body. Deep in her heart, Cathy knew this was her last hurrah at a second chance in life.

Cathy cuddled into her husbands arms for a loving night of sleep. She wondered how a man could satisfy one woman for so long. She thought it would be easier to satisfy a hundred or a thousand different women, but for six years he satisfied her every physical and emotional need. Even though he put on 25 pounds since they met and was graying quickly for a 48 year-old man, just his smell or the sound of his voice was enough to satisfy her. "It must be love," Cathy mumbled and drifted off to sleep.

They met while she was waiting tables in the obscure town of Jericho. The locals were mostly ranchers and cattlemen that journeyed to the small town for supplies. Cathy didn't recall seeing him when he began to eat at the diner, he blended in with the other cattlemen and hired hands. He later told her he used to dine at the counter until he noticed a gorgeous blond and found out where her stations were. Their relationship began with the canonical conversation between customer and waitress and progressed as they got to know one another. When he asked her to accompany him to a movie one day, she quickly turned him down, scared of her checkered past. She reflected on his proposition when she arrived home that evening and realized she didn't even know his name. He was very handsome, in an average sort of way, with nice features and a good smile. She knew he was not from Texas by his accent and suspected he relocated from somewhere up north. She reconsidered her position and decided she had earned an air of respectability. She had been clean for three years and had not jumped into bed with any of the locals; she was perceived as a nice lady. Every morning during the ensuing three weeks he asked her out after he finished a hearty breakfast. Although he seemed sincere and was very polite, Cathy continued to graciously turn him down (graciously because he was her best tipper, always two dollars for a $4.50 breakfast). One day, out of the blue, he changed his modus operandi and requested a second order of pancakes.

"You keep eating like that and you're going to lose all those muscles," Cathy said. He smiled.

"You like my muscles?" Realizing she was caught off guard, Cathy jokingly said,

"Of course, what all-American girl doesn't like a man with a firm body." He gently touched her hand as she refilled his coffee cup.

"Listen, let's go to the movies." Cathy didn't reply. He broke the silence with more charm than all the men Cathy ever met put together. "I'll even pay for the tickets," he offered, with a broad smile. Cathy laughed and strolled back to the kitchen to put in his second order of hot cakes, she was still chuckling to herself when she returned with the second stack.

"I don't even know your name," Cathy said sheepishly, as she placed the plate on the table.

"Roger Brown," he said.

Cathy and Roger dated for a month or so, usually catching a movie, bowling, or strolling the art galleries in Austin. She was swept away. He did not shower her with gifts, just an occasional rose; but he listened and seemed to understand her. It was not what he said or what he did, but just his being. Two things were becoming obvious to Cathy: one, she was falling fast for this Roger Brown, and two, he was the worst cattle rancher she ever saw. Cathy noticed whenever she brought the subject of ranching up he became very attentive, as if to learn something.

"You don't have a clue what you're doing," she told him poignantly over ice cream one night.

"You're right," he said, "but I'll get the hang of it."

"You'll go broke long before that," she said, as she wiped some butter pecan ice cream from his lip.

"Money is the least of my problems."

"I thought you were in the military. They don't make enough to operate a large ranch for very long."

"Oh, I see, truth and consequence time," Roger said. A blanket of silence fell over their conversation.

"I really appreciate you not pressuring me on the S and P words," Cathy said. Roger popped the bottom of his ice cream cone in his mouth and stared off through the orange neon lights in the parlor window.

"S and P," Roger said, drawing out his words. "Let's hold off on the S word for now and have a little discussion on the P word. P is for past, right?" Cathy, frightened that the man who regenerated her life was going to discover the bad and ugly of her world and embark on the beginning of the end, nodded her head. "Everyone has a past. Some things we are very proud of and other things we are not so proud of." Roger took her hand. "The past, in my opinion, is embodied of guilt. Guilt for the bad things we did to ourselves or others. I believe guilt is a wasted emotion and I also believe you and I are basically good people. Hindsight is 20/20 and it's easy to look back and judge errant decisions we made; however, at the time we made them we believed they were right." Roger paused and sipped his water. "Once you reflect and learn from your decisions it's time to go on. What's done is done." Roger paused to see if Cathy was still with him. He looked into her clear-colored eyes and saw she was hanging on his every word. "So you see, the past is immaterial to me. Whether I've learned from it or not, it's behind me and I can't change it. As for your past, it's exactly that, your past. We never have to talk about it, or if it makes you feel better, we can talk about it. There's nothing you could tell me that would change the way I feel about you, your past has absolutely nothing to do with our future."

"Maybe someday I'll talk about it, I've had a rough road," Cathy said, her eyes filling with tears. "And the same for you, if you ever need an ear, you know." Cathy was taken back by Roger's abrupt response.

"I'll never talk about my past, only that I inherited enough money to run 100 ranches. About the 'S' word, I gather that means sex," Roger ended. Cathy smiled.

"Yes, you've been a real gentleman. I needed that and appreciate it."

"Well, I hate to disappoint you, but I'm saving myself for marriage."

"Oh, yeah, right!" Cathy said, laughing. She loved the way he always said the right thing. "When was that sailor, 25 years ago?"

"I was in the army," Roger said, "but I was thinking about having sex with you next Saturday night."

"I thought you were saving yourself for marriage army boy," Cathy retorted, in a flirtatious manner. Roger smiled. Cathy looked down at the small ice cream parlor table, next to her left hand was the most beautiful engagement ring she had ever seen. The sex on Saturday night was sensational.

2

The construction of the eight bedroom house Roger designed was completed by their first anniversary. The house, with its great white pillars and railed decks surrounding each story, gave the grounds a central point of focus. The interior was part modern, part Early American and part Roger and Cat. The large, practical kitchen had an adjacent breakfast solarium with a retractable ceiling to take advantage of the temperate Texas climate. The spacious family room was furnished with a semi-circular white leather sectional and free-form malachite coffee table. Twenty-five inch flat screen televisions hung in each corner, and a remote control state-of-the-art entertainment center (which included a laser disc system and personal computer) dropped from nowhere in the center of the room. The master bedroom was large and luxurious. A huge circular bed graced the middle of the room and a breakfast nook on the eastern wall with floor to ceiling windows welcomed the sun each morning. On the opposite wall, French doors opened to a sitting room that had a fully stocked bar and entertainment system. An oversize black leather sofa sat in front of an 8x12 foot Polaroid glass window, providing a picture perfect view of the setting Texas sun beyond the landscaped gardens. When the weather was nice the window slid into the wall and was replaced with a nearly invisible insect net. The outdoor pool, hot tub, and changing house were located on the north side of the property. Beyond the white marble chips surrounding the pool was desolate, dry, dusty land leading to the oil fields in the Texas desert.

Cathy was very concerned about the financial state of the ranch during the first few years of their marriage. In addition to the cost of constructing and furnishing their new home, Roger hired a housekeeper and a few cowboys to look after the cattle. Every time she brought up her concerns Roger just smiled and said, "I told you, don't worry about money. It's all taken care of." Her anxiety diminished as time went on and they continued to live the life of Riley. Cat and Roger traveled to Europe for six weeks one year, took an extended second honeymoon in Hawaii the next, and made countless trips to Las Vegas on the spur of the moment for a little recreational gambling. Cat saw her husband lose over $125,000 playing blackjack one night, and win $275,000 playing craps the next. Losing never irritated Roger and winning never excited him, it was just a way of keeping score.

The ranch lost over $850,000 the third year they were married. When their accountant in Austin informed Roger of the figure he nodded his head and instructed him to start purchasing all available acreage adjacent to the ranch. Over the next six months Roger acquired an additional 235,000 acres, bringing the total acreage of the ranch to over 500,000. The cost of the expansion, after real estate and transfer taxes, commissions and insurance, was $50,000,000. Immediately after the acquisition Roger changed his strategy. Instead of working 18 hour days when the calves were born, he sold 1800 of the 2000 head; keeping only the most fertile bulls and a barnful of cows. He began to lease acreage to other cattlemen and by the fifth year of their marriage over 80% of the land was producing income. Cathy was astonished when she learned the ranch showed a handsome profit of $1.5 million the following year. Roger was pleased because he was able to spend more time with Cat and Tris.

The Brown's slowly entered the social community and started attending goodwill benefits, where their contributions were appreciated and noticed. They sponsored high school football, a big item in Texas, with a large donation to one of Austin's local teams. Roger was rewarded with a membership in the Father's Club Alumni, even though he did not have a child attending the school. Cathy pursued her interest in reading and volunteered two days a week at an Austin library. The library's day care center gave four year-old Tris the opportunity to mingle with other children while Cathy got out of the house for a few hours. The news of their generosity spread quickly and invitations to a myriad of social functions poured in. The Brown's attended most of the affairs related to the arts and always dressed to impress. Cathy's days of shopping at Wal-Mart were definitely behind her. The only other social events the Brown's made an effort to attend were connected to the U.S. Armed Services, such as benefits for the Veteran's of Foreign Wars and disabled veterans. Most of the military functions were casual and arriving in jeans and a pick-up truck replaced the black tie and limousine. Roger was a good teacher in the area of social graces. Cathy quickly learned if someone was talking above her head to keep quiet and give the perception of interest, and if the conversation was at her level, to just be herself. It amazed Cathy how her husband could fly effortlessly between both worlds with the grace of an eagle soaring.

Sitting on the patio sipping a cup of coffee, Cathy thought about the love making of the night before while waiting for Roger and Tris. Every morning Roger would get down on his knees, crawl into Tris's room to wake her, and then let her ride him like a bronco before joining Cathy for breakfast. She smiled and reflected on a book she read about King Arthur, 'come to Texas and I'll show you Camelot.' Her daydream yielded to reality as Roger and Tris emerged from the house. It was a hot September morning and haze obscured the expansive horizon beyond the neatly landscaped shrubs and trees near the house. Roger had decided to keep 100,000 acres for their private use, with the cattle, barn, and other equipment almost two miles from the south side of the house.

"Are you going to the library?" Roger asked, as he kissed his wife and ran his hand along her rear end. Cathy swiped his hand away, afraid of being caught by the housekeeper or Tris.

"Yes, sir, and I'm taking my favorite girl with me," Cathy responded. "You're going to the Cattleman's Club for some business, right?"

"Yes ma'am. Those cattle ranchers want me to sign a ten year lease at a fixed rate," Roger said, cunningly.

"Well, that's only fair. You would want to know what your expenses for the land lease were," Cathy replied.

"I agree, and that's exactly what I want them to do," Roger said, as he picked up Tris and began to tickle her. Cathy was confused for a second and then looked at her husband in awe.

"That's brilliant! That means you'll know exactly what the income from the land is for ten years!"

"Yep." Roger planted a kiss on his daughter's face and returned her to her chair.

"Well, I have some news," Cathy said, directing her words to Tris.

"What, Mommy?" Tris asked eagerly.

"Well, there will be a new little girl at the day care today, a special little girl," Cathy said, in the sing-song voice mothers use to their small children.

"What makes her special? And what's her name?" Tris asked, with a twang of a southern accent.

"Well, her name is Sara, and her grandfather was a U.S. Senator and the Vice President of the United States about 12 years ago."

"Wow! He was almost President," Tris exclaimed. Cathy turned to Roger to share her parental excitement over the announcement of the special girl joining Tris's day care program. For a fraction of a second his eyes held a dead cold stare, she could feel him calculating and evaluating every syllable she spoke. Cathy had never seen that cold glare in his eyes during the six years they were together and it sent macabre chills down her spine.

"That should be nice," Roger said, quickly recomposing himself. The family finished their breakfast without any further conversation and Roger went upstairs to shower and dress while Cathy and Tris cleared the table.

Dressed in a dark, olive green suit, Roger gave the lease agreement one final look before placing it in his briefcase. He stopped in the family room and gave Cathy a kiss as he left for the Cattleman's Club. She embraced him in a long, passionate hug and told him how sexy he looked.

"I'll make the meeting quick if you take a half-day at the library. We can do the nasty and have the rest of the day to ourselves in the pool. A porterhouse on the grill, a bottle of dago red, more nasty. . . " Roger added, with more than a casual invitation.

"Love to, but no can do. We don't have any coverage today, love, I'll take a rain check though," Cathy responded, as she gave her husband a final peck on the lips. As he stepped out the door he hesitated and turned back to Cathy,

"Be careful, Cat." His concern for her and Tris was normal, but those cold, glaring eyes. . . .

Roger's negotiations with the members of the Cattleman's Club culminated in a five year lease for 200,000 acres. The contract was shorter than he wanted, but the per acre revenue was 30% higher than he expected. Since Cat declined his invitation for an afternoon rendezvous, Roger had lunch at the club with the other ranchers after business was concluded. The 14 ounce porterhouse steak, Texas fries, baked tomato and Coor's Light were good, and filling. Roger's waistline extended well past his belt, which had run out of holes. As he walked out of the restaurant he decided he would take the family to Orlando for a three day celebration, and start a strict diet and workout regime when they returned. Cat's words were kind when she said the extra 25 pounds were only more to love, he knew it was really closer to 50 pounds and he never felt so out of shape. Roger pulled onto the highway and flipped on the radio to see what the market was doing on his way home. Roger felt the blood drain from his face as he caught the end of a report about the kidnaping of former Vice President B.J. Day's granddaughter at a library in Austin. He picked up the cell phone and speed dialed the library as the newscaster recapped the story and reported that shots were fired and there were casualties. Busy signal. Roger clicked the phone back on and called the ranch. He asked their housekeeper if she heard from Mrs. Brown, to which she replied, 'no.' Roger was still on hold with the Austin Police when he arrived at the library ten minutes later. He dropped the phone on the passenger seat and hurried to the yellow police tape as his old instincts took over. He asked one of the officers who was in charge and was directed to a sergeant in dress blues.

"Sir, my name is Roger Brown," The sergeant looked at him with an eye of suspicion. "my wife is the librarian here and my daughter was attending the day care." It took all Roger's emotional strength and character to keep cool and calm.

"Let me see some I.D.," the sergeant said. Roger removed his wallet and presented his Texas driver's license. "Come with me."

The sergeant explained the FBI had taken over the investigation as he escorted Roger inside the building. As they entered the library Roger's eyes scanned the room, noticing everything and everyone. He saw a bullet hole in the glass of the inner door, books scattered over the tables and floor, and drying drops of blood on the rug leading out the door. He began to tremble, thinking it could be Cat or Tris's blood, but regained control in a millisecond. The library was filled with Austin's finest and there was a group of suits conversing at the entrance to the day care center. The men stopped talking and turned toward Roger and the sergeant as they approached.

"This is Roger Brown, husband of the librarian. Mr. Brown, this is Special Agent Taylor." The two men shook hands as the sergeant finished his introduction and then began to speak concurrently, neither hearing what the other was saying. Agent Taylor held up his hands to signal Roger to let him start.

"Sir, your wife was wounded severely during the kidnaping of Vice President Day's granddaughter," the FBI agent said. Roger fought back his tears.

"Is she dead?"

"No sir, she was taken to LBJ Memorial, but I stress her wounds were very severe."

"How about my daughter?" Roger asked.

"None of the children other than Vice President Day's granddaughter were harmed." A sense of relief rushed over Roger.

"Where is she?"

"The children have been transported to a gymnasium about a mile away. The Red Cross is there and they're being entertained by some circus clowns." Agent Taylor paused and looked solemnly at Roger, "She's being well looked after sir, I suggest you get to LBJ as soon as possible. Send a family member to pick up your daughter between 7:00 p.m. and 9:00 p.m., the sergeant will give you the address. Go to your wife, she's the one who needs you now."

The sergeant offered to drive Roger to the hospital and asked for his keys. They were escorted by a cruiser with lights and sirens blazing. Roger sat in quiet reflection, envisioning what took place, and forced himself not to think of the worst case scenario. He knew someone on the inside had to be involved. Even though the Secret Service does not protect grandchildren of former vice presidents, certain protocol is followed and local officials are informed of their whereabouts. He theorized a crew of five or six would be needed to execute the kidnaping, including at least one woman as an unobtrusive signal on the inside. Optimally, four would storm the building and one would wait in the vehicle, probably a mini-van. The first two entrants would head straight for the library counter, take out whoever was at the desk, and disable any surveillance equipment and phone lines. 'I'll skin those two alive,' Roger thought. The other two would rush the day care, one quieting any adult threats and the other, probably with a picture in hand, searching for the former V.P.'s granddaughter.

Roger's speculations were interrupted by silence when they arrived at the hospital and the sirens ceased. The sergeant escorted Roger through the emergency room entrance. As the two men approached the registration window, shouts of "we're losing her! we're losing her!" came from inside a cubicle in the trauma center. Roger was overcome by a sickening numbness as the sergeant inquired about Cathy. He saw three people exit the cubicle where the shouts were coming from. Their seafoam green scrubs were saturated with dark, crimson blood. "Too much blood loss," one said, "she probably never would have come out of the coma even if we could have stabilized her."

Roger was sure he was going to have a second look at his lunch when he felt the sergeants hand on his shoulder.

"Your wife is in the operating room. They don't think the lady in charge of the day care is going to make it."

"She didn't," Roger said.

"Is there anyone I can call for you? Anything you need?" the sergeant asked.

"No, no, you've been great." The sergeant clipped a 'visitor' pass to Roger's lapel and slipped his keys into his suit coat pocket.

"Go to the desk on the third floor and they'll keep you informed about your wife. I have to go now." They shook hands and Roger thanked him for his help. "I hope everything works out for the best Mr. Brown."

Roger entered the elevator at the far end of the sterile hall and pushed #3. He glanced at his watch and took note that it was 2:06 p.m. The nurse at the desk checked her clipboard and informed Roger that Cat had been in surgery for almost an hour. She directed him to the family waiting room and said the doctor would speak with him once she was out of surgery. The small room was painted hospital white and smelled of rubbing alcohol. There were six chairs positioned around the walls and a table, stacked with year-old periodicals, in the middle of the room. Two of the chairs were occupied by an elderly black couple who had a look of despair on their faces. Roger stared out the small window (that had a view of the hospital parking garage) for a few minutes and then paced for a while. He finally removed his jacket and settled in a chair across from the melancholy couple. They nodded at one another, understanding neither wanted any part of conversation.

Roger's focus shifted to the kidnappers. If Cathy was in the operating room for an hour, that would make it 1:00 p.m. He estimated it was a ten minute ambulance ride from the library to the hospital and another thirty minutes or so before the scene would have been discovered and the police arrived. Roger judged the raid on the library probably took place around noon. That made sense, the structure in the day care center would be at its lowest point, with three and four year-olds choosing between orange juice and milk. Roger was convinced someone working at the day care center, or the library, had to be in on the kidnaping. He closed his eyes and visualized the scene. The bullet hole in the inner glass door was small, probably an ouzi or similar automatic weapon. The fact that the target was the grandchild of a former United States Vice President led Roger to believe the motive was political, not monetary. Former Vice President Day was wealthy, but not super-rich, and his political views were very conservative, approaching right-wing extremism.

The former Vice President came from a wealthy Texas family. His father was a wildcat oil driller who struck it rich by bringing in some wells in the early 1920's. The elder Day parlayed his small fortune into a drilling company and retained the rights to the six wells. The family's fortune doubled when the senior Day took advantage of the stock market crash of 1929. Before his death he granted three trusts, one for each of his children, funded with the stock and income from the drilling company. The Day children were left in healthy financial condition, with each trust valued at approximately $125 million. The inheritance, from Roger's point of view, was the only success the former Vice President ever had. He was a horrid businessman, and blundered at over a dozen endeavors from drilling to banking. Feeling the pressure of failing at every entrepreneurial adventure, the Harvard graduate became intrigued with the idea of using his name and fortune to assist him in the political arena. On the advice of his wife, Isabel, Day decided to run the diplomatic gauntlet. He won the first election he entered and served two successive terms as a United States Congressman before losing his third. The loss was attributed to a scandal involving kickbacks on federal land deals, and although Day was never convicted, the shadow of the affair cast a dark cloud over his political momentum. The year following the loss of his Congressional seat was the lowest point of the former Vice President's life and he succumbed to depression. Four years after his defeat, the powers to be convinced Day to re-enter the political arena and run for the United States Senate. The party provided a professional spin doctor to reconstruct

Day's image. His public persona changed from that of a rich kid with a silver spoon, to that of a John Wayne character; always atop a horse and wearing a white hat. The political public relations expert taught Day that less was more and he became an expert at using simple analogies to reach the people. He won the Senate seat easily.

Unbeknownst to the newly elected Senator from Texas, the powers to be viewed him as their pawn. They saw a power-hungry failure who would do just about anything to prove he was more than just a beneficiary to a trust fund. The marriage of the Senator and the inner loop of Washington begat opportunity. Day voted and lobbied for the people who thrust him back into office like a puppet on a string. Four years later the Senator was rewarded with the position of Director of the FBI. He served as Director for the Bureau for two years before being appointed as the United States Ambassador to Great Britain. He jetted around the world for three years while the party recaptured the White House, then he was reassigned as the head of the National Security Agency.

When the party lost the White House they encouraged Day to run for President. He did well in the primaries and finished second, as planned, to the party's first choice. The powers to be knew Day didn't have what it took to be President, but he was a proven political puppet to place in the #2 position. The #1 pick was from the northeast section of the country, so Day was the logical choice for V.P. to help the party carry Texas and the southern states. The plan came off without a hitch. During the second year of his first term, the President appointed Day to chair a committee overseeing the CIA and NSA. Once again, the credulous Vice President was under the impression he was being rewarded for his loyalty. Day's appointment to the special committee turned out to be his Waterloo as scandals erupted near the end of the administration's second term. Although the Vice President was naive to allegations of the CIA dealing with terrorists for profit during covert operations, he was held accountable in the eye of the public. The smoky cloud of the terrorist scandal tipped the scales in favor of Day's opponent the following November in the closest Presidential election in the history of the United States. Day concluded the opposing party set him up for the fall with the terrorist scandal; oblivious to the reality that the powers to be decided it was time to have the other party control the White House and serve their hidden agenda.

Roger realized he was analyzing the days events to take his mind off the real matter at hand, and concluded with the thought that the ransom note from the kidnappers would express their motives. He had fallen into such deep thought about the possible suspects and their motives, he didn't even realize the elderly couple was gone. He looked at his watch and saw it was 6:15 p.m. Roger sauntered out to the nurses station to see if there was any news. He introduced himself to the new nurse on duty and she informed him his wife was still in the operating room, she was aware he was waiting, and the doctor would be with him as soon as Cathy was out of surgery. He returned to the waiting room, unable to decide if the fact that she was still in surgery was a good sign or a bad sign. He fought back his emotions and decided to think the best. He would wait until 8:15 p.m. before leaving to pick up Tris. Roger had no idea what he was going to tell her, he'd cross that bridge when he came to it.

The minutes passed like hours and Roger had lost his ability to concentrate. Alone in the small vacuous room, his only thoughts now were of his wife. He had been with many women and thought he had been in love on a couple occasions, but in retrospect, he had no idea what love was until he met Cat. At 7:40 p.m. the door to the family waiting room opened.

"Mr. Brown?" the woman inquired.

"Yes," Roger replied, jumping up out of his chair.

"I'm doctor Francis." Roger's first thought when the brownish-blond haired woman entered in her mauve-colored scrubs was that she resembled actress Glen Close. As she began to speak, with a hint of an British accent, Roger's instincts began to tingle. He knew this was a person he could trust.

"How's my wife?" Roger asked quickly. The doctor led him back to his chair and she sat in the one next to it.

"I've upgraded her condition from critical to guarded." Roger let out a sigh of relief. "Listen, she's not out of the woods yet, there are multiple complications. Your wife was shot four times. One bullet passed through her left side without incident, the second bullet entered her lower abdomen and did irreparable damage to her uterus. We had to perform a radical hysterectomy. Mr. Brown, your wife cannot have any more children." The doctor paused to make certain Roger understood. When he nodded his head she continued, "The third bullet shattered her right cheek bone, but deflected away from the orbit, the bones around the eyes, and the brain. The facial damage is not as bad as it sounds and reconstructive surgery after her recovery can restore her appearance. The fourth bullet entered the right side of her chest near the nipple of her right breast. This wound caused the most concern, it shattered two ribs and fractured and lodged in a third. The mass of bone fragments damaged the lower lobe of her lung beyond repair. We removed the shattered ribs and the lower lobe of her right lung." Dr. Francis saw the concern on Roger's face and tried to reassure him. "She can live a normal life, many people do. A baseball player who had a lung removed some years back returned to play professional baseball after recovery," the doctor said, ending on a positive note.

"Johnny Bench," Roger said.

"Excuse me?"

"Johnny Bench was the baseball player you were referring to."

"Oh, good, then you understand." Roger nodded and waited for the other shoe to drop. "I do have a major concern, your wife needs rest to give her body a chance to heal and adjust to functioning with a reduced lung capacity."

"I don't see that as a problem," Roger stated.

"Well, when we brought her out of the anesthesia she became hysterical, screaming, 'Don't put me to sleep! I need to talk to my husband!' This happens occasionally in trauma cases, but she went ballistic and even tried to get off the table. I'm extremely concerned about the extensive internal sutures tearing and internal bleeding. She only calmed down after I swore on my children's lives that I was going to get you."

"Let's go," Roger said.

Cathy was still in the recovery room when Roger was led to her bed. One of the nurses told Dr. Francis that it didn't appear Cathy did any damage during her outburst. Roger had seen more mangled bodies than he cared to recall, but the sight of Cat, with bandages over the right side of her face and tubes in her nose, arms, chest and belly took his wind for a second.

"Hi Cat," Roger said. Cathy turned toward him and tried to get up. Roger and one of the nurses quickly put their hands on her shoulders and lowered her back to the bed.

"Roger," Cathy said in a raspy voice, "Tris, Tris is the. . . ." Thinking his wife feared for their daughter's life, Roger tried to comfort her.

"Tris is fine. She's fine." Roger tried to explain Tris was at the gym with the Red Cross, but his words only seemed to fuel Cathy's fury. She grabbed the side rail of the bed and flailed at her husband's arm. She gasped from the pain as Roger again lowered her back to the bed. Cathy maintained a vice-like grip on his arm and Roger moved closer to prevent her from doing any more damage.

"Listen, you don't understand. I saw the people who shot me take Tris away. She called for me."

"They kidnaped Vice President Day's grandchild, Tris is fine." Her grip tightened and she looked straight into Roger's eyes.

"Tris and the other girl look a lot alike. They were both wearing Mickey Mouse t-shirts. They took Tris." Cathy's eyes and Roger's instincts told him it was true. "Yes, yes. I don't know what you did before and I don't give a fuck, but I want to see more of that glare in your eyes. Promise me you'll bring our baby back." Roger nodded his head and Cathy's grip relaxed as the nurse injected a sedative into her IV. She looked up at her husband and smiled at the death she saw in his cold, steel eyes as she drifted out of consciousness.

3

When Roger arrived back at the library at 9:15 p.m, the Austin police had been joined by the FBI and three television news vans. He glided through a small crowd toward the yellow police tape and spied the sergeant who drove him to the hospital.

"Sarge!" Roger caught his attention and the uniformed officer walked over to the tape.

"How's your wife?" he asked.

"She's going to make it," Roger answered.

"Good, I'm glad for you," the sergeant responded.

"Listen, do you think you could get me the number of that FBI agent, Taylor?"

"Is it about the kidnaping?"

"Yes," Roger said.

"Come with me, he's still here." The sergeant lifted the yellow 'Do Not Cross' tape for Roger to duck under. As the two men climbed the steps to the library, Roger commented,

"Extra suits, looks like Secret Service." The sergeant just raised his eyebrows. He escorted Roger to Agent Taylor, who was standing with more of the Secret Service suits. The sergeant reintroduced Roger and excused himself.

"How's your wife?" Taylor asked.

"She's going to be fine," Roger replied.

"How can I help you?"

"May I have a moment alone with you?" Roger asked, in a charming, yet commanding tone. The FBI agent hesitated a moment and then said,

"Sure, let's walk over here." He guided Roger away from the suits and crime scene people gathered at the day care center. "What's up?"

"Any breaks on who did this? Or ransom notes?" Roger asked.

"I'm not at liberty to discuss an ongoing investigation Mr. Brown," Taylor replied dryly.

"What if I told you that the kidnappers did not kidnap the former Vice President's grandchild?" Roger asked.

"I would ask you how you know that information and where you received it from," Taylor replied.

"My wife," Roger answered. "She saw the kidnappers take my daughter as they made their exit. Is there a ransom note yet?" Roger demanded. The FBI agent was taken back by Roger's presence and his knowledge of the case.

"Off the record," Taylor said.

"Okay, we'll do it your way," Roger replied.

"We received a ransom tape about 45 minutes ago, Fed-Ex of all things," Taylor said, with a note of disgust in his voice.

"I know you can't discuss the information on the tape, but if it was for money nod your head." Taylor shook his head slightly, indicating 'no'. "Then it's political," Roger stated. The agent confirmed his statement with a single nod. Roger's adrenaline began to flow and his instincts took over. "Why all the Secret Service?"

"Old man Day is in the day care center," Taylor answered.

"Do me a favor, take me to him," Roger commanded.

"Why in God's name should I do that?" Taylor asked, indignantly. Roger took a deep breath, he knew the moment called for finesse, not ferocity.

"First, if it gets out that the kidnappers don't have his grandchild, my daughter is as good as dead. Then these terrorists, and they are terrorists, will go underground until they set up their next victim."

"I thought of that," Taylor said.

"Second, he knows me." Taylor believed this man, he did not know why, but he did.

"Come with me." The two men walked toward the day care center. "How do you know they're terrorists?" Taylor asked.

"The bullets. Ouzi. The terrorist weapon of choice," Roger answered, flippantly.

"Who the fuck are you?" Taylor asked, obviously annoyed.

"You really don't want to know," Roger answered. "How many people know the kidnappers didn't get the Vice President's granddaughter?"

"I don't know, seven or eight. The VP, the kid, her parents, a couple Secret Service men, me, a Red Cross employee. . . . Why?" Taylor asked.

"Damage control," Roger replied, obviously controlling the situation. "Do you have a business card?" The FBI agent removed a brass case from his suit and offered a card to Roger as they approached former Vice President Day. "Is your line secure?" Roger asked.

"Why in God's name would you want to know that!" Taylor exploded. He stopped walking ten feet from the VP and looked at Roger with a 'this better be good or all deals are off' expression. Roger was comfortably set on cruise control thanks to his reliable instincts of years gone by. He turned to Taylor as he slid the agent's business card in his pocket.

"This is my daughter. I will do anything and everything to make certain that not a hair on her head is disturbed. I think, or rather I pray, that you are half as intelligent as you look and realize that I am not what I appear to be. Let's just say that since I retired from my previous occupation I'm no longer in the loop and you are my contact, or should I say my conduit." Taylor had been in the bureau for 15 years, shot a person dead, and took one in the shoulder seven years ago during a raid in Dallas. He knew how fear and adrenaline could be used to one's advantage, but this guy just plain scared him.

Special Agent Joseph Ryan Taylor was born in Providence, Rhode Island and reared in Durham, North Carolina. His father was a professor of Economics at Duke University and their family was modeled after the Cleaver's. Taylor attended North Carolina State University, enrolled in ROTC, and entered the United States Army at age 21. His degree in criminal justice and armed forces experience as a military police officer earned him a stint at the Pentagon as an attache for a full bird colonel in charge of army intelligence for NATO in Poland. After serving six years in the army, Captain Taylor left the military and pursued his life-long dream of becoming a federal officer. He was accepted at the FBI Academy, where he met his wife Bernadette, and managed to conceive two children during the few hours he was not working.

His hard work paid off at age 38 when he was promoted to Chief Hostage Negotiator of the Austin Bureau office. In addition to a substantial salary increase, the new position would be less demanding on his time and he would finally have the opportunity to focus on his wife and daughters. But before he received his next paycheck, Bernadette asked him for a divorce. Taylor tried to explain how things were going to be different once he settled into his new position, but it was too little, too late.

"While you were out playing Elliot fucking Ness, I fell in love with some one else; who happens to love me more than his job. It's over." The words penetrated Taylor's heart like the sharp steel of a knife.

"Who is he?"

"The life insurance agent." Taylor submerged himself in his work to avoid facing his feelings of emotional failure after their separation. He volunteered to help other field offices to gain experience and keep busy. Over the next five years he handled nine cases without losing a hostage and earned an accommodation from the Bureau. During his stay at the Pentagon he heard about deep-cover spooks who would do whatever was necessary to accomplish their mission; he had an eerie feeling he just met one.

"Vice President Day, this is Mr. Roger Brown. His wife works at the library and was shot during the episode," Taylor said. Day was a man of 80 years and although his frame of 5'10" carried a hefty load of 200 pounds, he was still full of vim and vigor and was regarded as one of the most powerful men in Texas.

"Mr. Brown, I understand we're neighbors of a sort, our ranches connect. Sorry to meet you under such grave circumstances." As Day extended his hand their eyes met and the air in the room turned Alaskan cold. "Oh my God, it's you!" Day said. "You're not a part of this are you?"

"My wife is fine Mr. Vice President, thank you for your concern," Roger said, coldly.

"I'm truly sorry for her pain," Day said.

"I need you to do something for me."

"Why should I? You almost ruined a nation!" the VP retorted.

"I guess that's why I have all those medals," Roger countered.

"Semantics. What do you want?" the Vice President snapped.

"I need you to announce that the kidnappers have your granddaughter."

"Why in Sam Houston would I do a thing like that!" he barked, as he turned and glanced across the room at his granddaughter.

"If you don't make the announcement the kidnappers will kill my daughter as sure as we're talking."

"Why should I help you? You cost me the Presidency," the old man said bitterly.

"We both know that's a bunch of bullshit. I did your dirty work for years and you owe me. I can still be a very large thorn in your side." The old man was silent in thought for a few seconds and then said,

"I'll make a statement, but I'll only play your little charade for 24 hours, you fuck."

"Use the Secret Service to get the girl out of here and make it right with her parents. I need 72 hours."

"Well too fucking bad, you're only getting 24. And you can stick your thorn up your ass!" Day abruptly turned away from Roger and went over to explain the situation to his daughter and son-in-law. Roger stepped toward Taylor and asked,

"Does that number reach you 24 hours a day?"

"Yeah, it does. What are you going to do?" Taylor asked, now more impressed with Brown than afraid.

"With your help, I'm going to find my daughter," Roger answered. "Do you have a list of library and day care employees?"

"Yes." He watched Roger snatch the list from his hand as he removed it from his suit coat pocket.

"Thanks, I'll be in touch." Roger disappeared through the door of the day care center, leaving the FBI agent standing among the miniature desks in bewilderment.

4

Assistant Chief of Staff, Ellis Grady's phone rang in the west wing of the White House. The west wing, the working wing, housed the Oval Office and hundreds of employees. "Grady," he answered, immediately picking up a pen and scribing his personal version of shorthand on a note pad. The digital readout on his phone showed 10:02 p.m. when he hung up and pressed the speed dial button to ring the Chief of Staff at home.

"The Sullivan residence," the housekeeper answered.

"Hello, Myra. How are you?" Grady was polite to everyone; he understood that one never knows when he is going to need a favor.

"Mr. Grady, fine, and yourself?"

"Very well. Is the lord and master of the house about?"

"Oh, Mr. Grady, if I was 20 years younger!" the housekeeper teased. "I'll go get Mr. Sullivan right away."

"Thank you, Myra." Grady had worked for Chief of Staff, Thomas Sullivan since their man took control of the White House six years ago. He was still trying to make sense of what the Secret Service told him about the events in Austin when Sullivan got on the line.

"What is it Ellis?" Chief of Staff, Sullivan snapped. He believed 12 hours a day was all the government was entitled to, and was a little peeved at being disturbed at his residence in Virginia. Sullivan knew Ellis Grady had a way of turning mid-size crises into large ones.

"That situation in Austin," Grady answered.

"You called me an hour ago and told me former Vice President Day's grandchild was not involved," Sullivan stated, obviously irritated.

"Yes, sir, that's still the situation," Grady reported.

"Then what!" Sullivan's patience had run out, especially since the situation involved former Vice President Day, who he did not like one iota.

"I just received a call from Treasury. They told me that the esteemed former VP made a statement to the media fifteen minutes ago pleading for the kidnappers not to harm his granddaughter."

"Why in the hell would he do that?" Sullivan asked.

"The Secret Service informed me it was at the request of the kidnaped child's father, a Mr. Roger Brown. The FBI believes a press announcement stating the kidnaped child is not the former vice president's would abate their chances to catch the kidnappers, and that the child's death would be eminent."

"I see," Sullivan said, in a more concerned tone. "Who is this Brown guy? And how many people are aware of the fact that this was a political kidnaping? And how the fuck did this Brown guy find out? We were supposed to keep a lid on the ransom tape."

"I don't know who he is or how many people know the contents of the ransom tape, but the man from Treasury told me that the Secret Service reported Brown and Day had a conversation at the day care. He said Day gave the impression of knowing Brown and it was more of an argument than a conversation. Brown asked Day for 72 hours, but the Vice President said he held all the cards and was only giving him 24 before going public with the truth about his granddaughter." There was a moment of silence, then the Chief of Staff confirmed that CNN was still running the abduction of Day's grandchild as its lead story.

"Stay in your office and keep your line open, I'm going to discuss this with #1. I'll call you back."

Grady knew what was coming. He accessed another line and contacted the FBI, IRS, NSA, Treasury, and CIA for information on Roger Brown. He made the requests on the behalf of the

Chief of Staff and indicated he needed them handled on a haste basis, which, in their circle, meant six hours or less. Grady's private line rang as he hung up with the CIA.

"Yes, sir," Grady answered.

"#1 is not a happy camper, you know how he despises loose ends. He had an 11:00 a.m. press conference scheduled tomorrow to inform the nation that everything was status quo, but this cloak and dagger stuff put a fly in the ointment." Sullivan's tone had changed from annoyed to that of a man who just had a new asshole ripped by the President of the United States.

"I understand. I've already taken the necessary steps to research this Roger Brown," Grady reported.

"We'll meet in my office at 8:30 a.m. to review. Get to the FBI and the Treasury and get to the bottom of this mess," Sullivan ordered. "I want to make some sense out of this situation before we meet with #1." Sullivan hung up the phone and Grady called the kitchen for a pot of coffee, he knew he was in for an all-nighter.

The clock on the dash read 9:52 p.m. when Roger started his car. He picked up the cell phone and dialed the home of William Buck, another member of the Austin Father & Son Club, who owned a local television station. The station had been in Buck's family since it came on the air in the mid-sixties. It began as a UHF frequency and then picked up syndicated re-runs during the '70's and 80's. A few years ago, Buck signed a deal with the Fox network to carry nationally broadcast professional and collegiate sporting events and the station began to hold its own in the rating wars. The addition of a seasoned, top anchorman last fall launched Buck into the #2 position for the 6:00 p.m. and 11:00 p.m. newscasts. Roger knew Buck had made several above the board deals to become a managing partner in a newly established cable network in Austin, and he felt he was dealing with a man of integrity. He just hoped his instincts were right.

"Hello?" Bill answered.

"Bill, hi, this is Roger Brown."

"Roger, how's Cathy? I'm so sorry. I tried calling you earlier today when the report came in."

"She's going to be fine, thank you for your concern. Bill, I need you to do me a favor."

"Anything," Buck replied.

"Don't ask any questions, just meet me at your station as soon as possible."

"I'll be there in thirty minutes," Buck said, without hesitation.

'That worked well,' Roger thought, as he clicked off the phone. The T.V. station was in the general direction of his ranch and it would take him about a half-hour to arrive. Roger clicked the phone back on and dialed Irving Stein, an attorney out of Philadelphia who administered his personal trust. A female answered the phone and inquired who was calling. Roger identified himself and a minute later Stein was on the line.

"Mr. Brown, how are you?" Stein asked.

"Listen very carefully and do what I ask as soon as humanly possible," Roger ordered.

"Go ahead."

"Liquidate $150 million dollars from the trust. Of that $150 million, put $100 million in my personal checking account for the ranch, make $25 million payable to William Buck's television station in Austin. Reconstitute the financial identity of alias, David Coyle and transfer the remaining $25 million to his account. Be sure to reestablish Coyle's credit cards and identification documents." Stein repeated the instructions and advised Roger his requests would be completed by 8:00 a.m. He had dealt with Stein for over 25 years and the man never failed him. His final call was to his ranch to assure the housekeeper everything was okay. She read him the long list of well-wishers who called with concern for Cathy. Roger recognized all the names, which made him feel confident the kidnappers still believed they had the Vice President's granddaughter. He told her he would be home later and asked her to make some spaghetti with butter and leave it in the fridge for him.

As Roger pulled into Buck's television station he reflected upon his previous occupation. One of his tenets was never to trust anyone when he was working, but this time he knew he was going to have to bend that rule. He was sure Buck was a decent man, but he also knew he was a reporter at heart, thus, the $25 million. Buck was standing by the entrance to the station when Roger arrived. He met him with a firm handshake and asked if there was some place they could speak privately. Buck led Roger to his spacious, high-tech office, encircled with TV monitors. He showed Roger to a chair in front of his chrome and glass desk and asked, in a very serious tone,

"What's going on? You said Cathy was going to be alright."

"You have video equipment here, right?" Roger asked.

"Yes," Buck replied, "what does that have to do with anything?" Buck's no nonsense attitude gave Roger a sense that he would accede with his plan.

"As I told you, Cathy is going to be fine, they took real good care of her at the hospital. That's not the reason I asked you to meet me here. Your station, and I pray every other news station, it still reporting that former Vice President Day's granddaughter was kidnaped, right?"

"Yes," Buck replied, hanging on Roger's every word.

"I need to know that I can trust you. I feel that I can from our past association, but I need your word, as a gentleman, that what I am about to tell you will go no further than this room." Buck pushed his chair away from his desk, contemplated getting up, and changed his mind.

"As a gentleman, you have my word this is off the record. Something obviously has you by the balls." Roger went for broke.

"The reports that former Vice President Day's granddaughter was kidnaped are false," Roger said.

"How do you know that?" Buck asked.

"Because Cathy told me she saw who the kidnappers really abducted; it was my daughter, Tris. Through an FBI agent, named Taylor, I convinced the former Vice President to make that press release to buy time." Roger looked at Buck for a response.

"I'm so sorry, Roger."

"The transcendent problem is their ransom tape is strictly political. As soon as the kidnappers realize Tris has no value to them, they will kill her. The problem is complicated by the fact that the gracious former VP is only willing to play along for 24 hours."

"What can I do to help?" Buck asked.

"First, keep your word. Second, I want you to videotape a message from me offering a reward to the kidnappers," Roger said.

"And what am I going to do with this video tape?" Buck asked. Roger wrote down Agent Taylor's name on a piece of Buck's note paper as he answered.

"If you don't hear that the case has been resolved from me or Taylor, and the other stations start reporting that there was a mistaken identity on the kidnaped child, I want you to run the video as long as you can. Tomorrow, around 8:00 a.m., there will be a retainer of $25 million in your station's account to run the broadcast. Run it every two hours, or as often as you think," Roger ended.

"Twenty-five million dollars will buy a lot of air time, and the national boys will run the broadcast over and over for ratings," Buck said.

"That's exactly what I want. God willing it will buy the FBI and I time to get Tris back.

"When do you want to do the video?" Buck asked.

"Now," Roger said.

"Okay, I'll film it myself." Buck stood and offered his hand. "You know, a lot of people speak highly of you; you're fair in business dealings and very generous to the less fortunate, but if this turns out to be a hoax of some sort you will have lost my friendship forever."

"It's not a hoax," Roger replied. The two men shook hands.

Roger sat behind the news desk and waited for Buck's signal.

My name is Roger Brown. This message is to the abductors of my daughter, Patricia Brown. By now you know she is not the grandchild of former Vice President Day. I am aware that your motives were of a political nature, but I am here to offer you $100 million for the safe return of my daughter. The money has been deposited in The First Bank of Austin and I will meet any requirements for method of payment, here or abroad, even in a country that has no extradition agreement with the United States. I am willing to do whatever is necessary for the safe return of my daughter. Please don't harm her.

After Roger reviewed the tape, Buck walked him to his car.

"You said the former Vice President is only going along for 24 hours. If he has his grandchild back, why not help your daughter?" Buck asked.

"To make a long story short, we have a past. The former Vice President and I have no love lost for one another. I think I can convince him to play along for 72 hours, but please, be alert and run the tape if necessary." As the two men parted, Buck assured him he would.

5

Roger arrived back at the ranch a little past 1:00 a.m. on Thursday morning. He found the spaghetti in the refrigerator, put a little extra butter on top of it, and popped it in the microwave while he grabbed a Pepsi and a fork. As he removed the plastic wrap from his dinner the teary-eyed housekeeper entered the kitchen. Roger embraced the 60 year old lady and told her Cathy was going to be alright. He kissed her on the cheek and retired to the basement, explaining he had some business to take care of before going back to the hospital.

The basement was the full size of the house and included an office, a play area for Tris, and a game room with a pool table and dart board. Roger's leather apportioned office was more reminiscent of a gentleman's library than a working office. He sat at his desk and inhaled the buttery spaghetti in less than a minute. He took a sip of his soda, locked the office door, and knelt down under the desk. Roger carefully removed four carpet tiles, exposing a trap door with a recessed combination lock. He dialed Cathy's birthday and removed the door from the floor. He grabbed his Pepsi, double checked the door, and descended the stairs leading to 20'x20' room of poured gray cement. Roger had given the builder $50,000 in cash to put in the hidden room and keep it off the plans submitted to the county for approval. The builder died two and a half years later of natural causes.

The room was filled with memorabilia from Roger's past. A rack of guns on one wall, a closet filled with uniforms and suits, state of the art listening devices, a make-up mirror with assorted wigs and mustaches, a collection of knives and wire cutters, and an assortment of drugs. A phone with a secure line (he made certain of that weekly) sat on a 4'x4' wooden table in the center of the room with one chair. He retrieved a couple amphetamines and sat at the table, sleep was out of the question. 'Let the hunt begin,' Roger thought. There was no middle ground, either he would see the safe return of his daughter, or he would die trying. He replayed the days events in his mind, searching for anything that may correlate to the kidnaping. Roger trusted his instincts, which always seemed to serve him well on a mission, and accepted the premise that there was someone on the inside at the library. He recalled the invitation he gave to his wife to do the nasty. 'What did she say?' Roger asked himself aloud. 'No can do, no coverage.' Who did Cat work with on Wednesdays? He reached inside his suit coat pocket and unfolded the list of library employees he took from FBI agent Taylor. Cat often spoke about the inner workings of the library during casual conversation over dinner, but more often than not, Roger only half listened and un-huhed his wife about the gossip. He tried to remember any names Cat mentioned and match them to the list, but he was drawing a blank and becoming frustrated. Roger knew the beginning of the journey to get his baby back was staring right at him, if only he could recognize it. Out of nowhere, he remembered Cat telling him about a girl in her early thirties who had no luck with men. He recalled he actually met her once while picking Cat up at the library and immediately understood why - she was one of the ugliest people he had ever seen. What did Cat say about her? He was angry with himself for patronizing his wife and not listening to the details of her gossip. He tried to compose a mental picture of her based on their single meeting, and put a name to her face. 'What the fuck was her name!' Roger started playing the alphabet game, Angela, Ann, Adrian, Amanda. . . . On his second time through he stopped at 'P.' 'Patricia, Pearl, Peg; Peg, that's it, Peg!' He scanned the list, but found no Peg. He reviewed it again and spied Margaret Short halfway down the page. 'Peg Short, Peggy Short,' he said aloud, convinced that was the lady Cat spoke of. He copied her address, birth date and social security number on a piece of paper and slipped it in his pocket.

Roger felt a rush of adrenaline as he gathered his equipment. He packed a few casual changes of clothes and one suit, with a matching tie, shoes and socks, in a small valet and sat it on the wooden table. Then he strapped on a shoulder holster containing a 9mm Glock and slipped a .22 in an ankle strap. Roger removed one of the knives from his collection and slid its nine inch blade into a leather casing on the shoulder holster. Finally, he retrieved a metal briefcase with a disassembled M-16 from the closet and set it on the table with a homing device and extra ammunition for the weapons. Roger sat at the make-up mirror and began the physical transformation to David Coyle, the alias he instructed Stein to bring back to life. FBI Agent Coyle's ID pictured a man about 40, completely bald, with a mustache. Outside of the additional weight Roger put on, he still looked identical to the photo. He knew the quickest way to cut through red tape on the street was to be in law enforcement. If questioned by any bystanders, the FBI cover would give him time to keep moving. He gathered Coyle's drivers license, passport, credit cards, $25,000 cash and his lock picking tools. Roger removed the Texas license plates from his late model Cadillac and replaced them with California tags. He put the suitcase containing the M-16 in the space above the spare tire and laid the valet in the trunk. His subconscious had been working overtime (or maybe it was the speed) and by the time he returned to his subterranean office he was 100% convinced that Peggy Short worked with Cathy on Wednesdays and Fridays.

Roger sat at the Shaker table and dialed the number of Charles Buehler. Beuhler was ageless, he was old when Roger first met him 30 years ago, and his life in politics spanned several different administrations. He served as the United States Ambassador to France and was the head honcho of both the CIA and NSA during his career. Beuhler had connections in just about every office in D.C., and was still viewed as the biggest power broker in the inner loop. There were even rumors that Beuhler knew who fired the fatal shot from the grassy knoll in 1963. Roger did not dislike Beuhler, that was hard to do, but he was very aware that Beuhler played his words carefully, always allowing himself an out. It was Beuhler, or actually Roger catching Beuhler recirculating money, that taught him how to make a profit off the cold war and introduced him to the clandestine world of black ops. To Roger's delight, Beuhler answered the phone. Even at this early hour of the morning Roger doubted Beuhler was asleep; people like him did not sleep much, too many nightmares about innocent lives.

"Hello?" Beuhler said.

"This is Galahad," Roger said, using his old code name.

"A character out of Andrew Lloyd Weber's most famous musical," Beuhler taunted.

"What are you talking about?"

"The Angel of Death, from the Phantom of the Opera. Are you going to be my Angel of Death, Galahad?" Beuhler questioned, in his annoying aristocratic voice.

"Maybe," Roger replied evenly.

"Good. You know me, I like the best of everything; so why not the best assassin of all times."

"Are you aware of the events in Austin?" Roger asked, aware Beuhler and former Vice President Day were in bed together on a lot of deals in the 80's.

"Is that your work Galahad? My, my, we are losing our touch! Oh, the years have a way of doing that to us. Let's see, you must be pushing 50," Beuhler goaded.

"You know better, I would have kidnaped the correct mark," Roger snapped. Beuhler hesitated slightly before responding.

"My, my, why am I the recipient of this new development?"

"You would have found out the truth in a few hours anyway," Roger said.

"Pray tell, whose little girl was kidnaped?" Roger was silent for a second.

"Mine, by mistake."

"You mean you had a child? I'll make a mental note of that. I'm sure the CIA would be very interested in her considering her lineage," Beuhler said. Roger was tiring of playing the old man's word games.

"All deals are off from seven years ago. My people are in place with all the necessary information and supporting documentation, including the disc."

"A deal is a deal Galahad. We kept our end and I must admit, up to this point, you've kept yours. What do you want?"

"I want you to use your influence wherever I need it to get my daughter back," Roger demanded.

"Your wish is my command," Beuhler replied.

"First, tell the White House who they're dealing with. Your asshole friend Day is threatening to go public in about 18 hours. Have them shut him up until I get my daughter back."

"Let it be said, let it be done," Beuhler replied.

"Second, there is an FBI agent named Taylor who was at the scene in Austin. I'm using him as my contact, make sure he gets everything he needs. And get the other officials away from the case."

"No problem. What do I get for my service?" Beuhler asked.

"Your continued anonymity from being one of the most evil men of the 20th century - and no painful visit from the Angel of Death." Roger hung up the phone.

David Coyle got in his Caddy and headed toward Austin. He had a vague idea where Peggy Short lived and hoped the confusion over the kidnaping kept the FBI from doing their preliminary interviews. He sped down the highway at over 100 mph, there was an unwritten rule in Texas- no other cars on the road, the sky's the limit. He arrived at the unsecured apartment complex of Peggy Short at 4:07 a.m. He aspired to be in and out by no later than 5:15 a.m., before dawn. He parked next to another Caddy, found the apartment, and picked the lock in less than five minutes. 'Like riding a bike,' he said to himself. Roger stepped inside the dark apartment and quietly shut the door. His instincts, and the smell in the apartment, told him Peggy Short was dead. He had smelled the unmistakable stench of death a hundred times over. Roger removed the Glock from its holster and began to walk around the perimeter of the apartment, checking each room to be certain he was alone. He knew the dead body of Peggy Short was the only other person in the apartment, but old habits die hard. When he reached the bedroom he saw the outline of a body partially slumped over the bed. He found the light switch, flipped it on, and dove to the floor. Silence. Roger knelt down next to the naked corpse and located two entrance wounds at the base of the skull. He recalled the day he met the woman at the library, just as ugly dead as she was alive, he thought. Roger estimated she had been dead one or two days, which meant she was killed prior to the kidnaping.

He began searching for clues that could lead him to Peggy Short's killer and his daughter's abductors. Short was obviously the person on the inside, and she was probably oblivious to the fact that she was helping to set up a kidnaping. Spooks and terrorists always used innocent people to accomplish their missions, and 99% of the time the innocent people never knew they were being used. Roger was as good as anyone at turning a place upside down searching for clues, but there were none. He glanced at his watch, 5:01 a.m. He returned to the bedroom and looked at the naked corpse. Naked. Sex? A diary? Cat's words came to mind, 'she's always had a problem with men.' 'No, no, this is it,' Roger said, as he noticed a computer atop a small table in the corner of the bedroom. He turned on the PC and reviewed her web page. He clicked on a button entitled 'For Me,' which brought up a password screen. Roger reached into his pocket and pulled out the paper containing the information he copied from the FBI list on Peggy Short. He entered her date of birth and, to his relief, the screen opened. Roger began to read her electronic diary. She met a man in his late 50's named Don Juan about four months ago. He was a gentleman, and didn't have sex with her until their fourth date. Peggy wrote very explicitly about the sex and was obviously a hopeless romantic. In the middle of August, Don Juan introduced her to five of his friends. There was a man called Jesus, from Don Juan's homeland of Spain, an Iranian named Kabiv, two Americans (George and Eric,) and a Puerto Rican named Illiana. It was obvious from the tone of her writing that she did not care too much for his friends. Roger learned that the one American, Eric, was a pilot and that the woman liked to brag about her sexual conquests with the five men, including Don Juan. Her last two entries were dated a week before the kidnaping. The first one told of Don Juan's proposal and their plans for a wedding in the spring. The final entry took a 180,

They think I'm stupid, all the questions about the people at the library. I know what they're up to. I know their headed for San Antonio, they just want the Fed's to think they're going to the border. I know they're headed to Boulder and Eric's flying them out of the country.

Roger knew he hit the mother load and had to concentrate to keep his adrenaline in check. He memorized the names and places and deleted the file, the last thing he needed was a couple of amateur FBI agents discovering the lead. Roger did not have to worry about his fingerprints, they were a gift from a dead man 27 years ago courtesy of the United States government. When he left the apartment at 5:51 a.m. the colorless light preceding the dawn had arrived. He had a good thought for Peggy Short as he quietly closed the door, at least she was the other 1%.

Roger decided he would head for San Antonio and try to pick up the kidnappers trail. The drive would give his subconscious a chance to work while Beuhler pulled the strings in D.C. He stopped for gas and breakfast around 8:00 a.m. and located a Fed Ex office. He sent a package same day delivery to Agent Taylor and made a mental note to call him later that afternoon, by then Beuhler should have had time to make Taylor the head Fed on the case.

6

"What do you mean there are no records of Roger Brown before seven years ago?" The President of the United states asked. President James Burke took the reins of the Oval Office six years prior, riding in on the saddle of the Day scandal. Burke was born and bred in southern Illinois and graduated from Northwestern University with a masters degree in political science. Burke accepted a position as political editor of Time Magazine, and found he truly enjoyed expressing his political views. At age 29, on a shoestring budget, he decided to run for Congress. Burke lost the election and failed at two subsequent attempts to enter the political arena, however, the exposure of the three elections created a public persona that laid the foundation for his political career. Burke was perceived as an honest man trying to do an honest job. He was self-critical, straight to the point, and gave the impression that although he was not perfect, he would do his best with integrity. It was that public perception that won him a seat in the United States Senate and, eventually, the Oval Office. Just as Chief of Staff, Sullivan was about to answer, the President's secretary buzzed in. Burke hit the intercom speaker,

"Yes."

"Sir, there's a Charles Beuhler here to see you. He stated it's an emergency." Beuhler's charm and influence was not loyal to any one party, country, or person. He was a man to be reckoned with and treated with the utmost respect.

"Send him in," Burke ordered. "And cancel that 11:00 a.m. press conference. I hate when my schedule gets all screwed up."

Both Chief of Staff, Sullivan and Assistant Chief of Staff, Grady nodded in agreement.

"Charles, how are you?" The President asked, walking out from behind his desk and shaking hands with the ancient power broker.

"Very well, Mr. President, and yourself?"

"Good, good. Some little problems here and there, but overall good," the President answered, sitting down with Beuhler on the first couch.

"Every time I step foot in this office I can feel my pulse rate rise," Beuhler commented. "One of those little problems would not be the situation in Austin, would it?" The President was a little taken back that Beuhler knew about Austin, but he was not shocked.

"Actually, yes," Burke replied. He introduced Sullivan, who had met Beuhler socially a few times, and Grady, who considered Beuhler his idol and made a bit of a fool of himself by expressing the same. The President knew Beuhler and former Vice President Day were friendly, but Beuhler had a lot of friends.

"Charles, I'm going to take you in my confidence. . ." Beuhler quickly cut the President off,

"I already know the kidnapper's don't have Day's grandchild."

"You spoke with Day?" Grady asked, getting a stern look from both Sullivan and the President.

"No, no, my boy, I was contacted by a man who you would know as Roger Brown," Beuhler stated. The other men were silent. "I would speculate that it was your job to research Roger Brown. Am I correct?" Beuhler asked, directing his words to Assistant Chief of Staff, Grady. Grady, in a hypnotic state of awe, had slipped onto the chair opposite the President and Beuhler. Sullivan was the last man standing.

"Yes, sir," Grady replied.

"Indulge an old man and tell me your fairy tale of Roger Brown," Beuhler stated. Grady looked at the President, who gave him a nod, and picked up his notes.

"Roger Brown is 48 years old, has a wife named Catherine and a daughter named Patricia. He resides at his ranch 40 miles west of Austin. The property is worth around $150 million and, from tax records starting seven years ago, he has a personal trust valued between $600 and $800 million. He leases about 80% of the ranch for income and turns a profit of two to three million dollars per year." Grady stopped and looked at the President, who nodded for him to continue. "He appears to be an upstanding citizen, no criminal record, not even a speeding ticket." Grady paused. "But there is no record of his existence prior to seven years ago, the man just seemed to appear out of thin air."

"Very good my boy, very good," Beuhler said.

"I gather your visit here this morning is to fill us in on this Brown man," the President remarked.

"That's part of the reason," Beuhler said.

"And the other part?" Chief of Staff Sullivan asked.

"Brown, as you know him, needs the cooperation of the White House to help him secure the safe return of his daughter. I'm sure that is everyone's first concern, and if it's not the White House's top priority then it should be, for you gentlemen do not have the slightest idea what you're dealing with," Beuhler replied, in a cold voice. The President knew the potentate emeritus of the inner loop did not make idle threats.

"Obviously, Charles, we don't have your experience with Mr. Brown. I would consider it a personal favor if you could shed some light on exactly what we are dealing with," the President begged.

"Oh, I will tell you a story, an unbelievable story - and if you're recording, this is just a fantasy story," Beuhler stated, knowing he had plausible deniability. "Once upon a time, I guess it was 1967 or '68, an orphan named Joseph Wilson was introduced into the United States Army. I believe he was 17 years old. He finished first at his boot camp, had great athleticism and he was already a master of the martial arts, we never did learn where he picked that up. . . ." Beuhler said, making the statement more for himself than the other three men. "An alert drill sergeant sent him to OIC school where he finished

45

first in his class again, showing great promise in the area of language. I believe he was fluent in three or four foreign tongues, but more importantly, his IQ was around 165 and the young man had the desire to learn. He was commissioned a second lieutenant, but chose to delay his promotion and go to paratrooper school with no rank; he indicated he wanted to be a Green Beret. The brass at the special forces snatched him up in a second and sent him to special forces training, where he proved himself the best once again. His psychological profile showed he was infatuated with the John Wayne movie "The Green Beret" and he exhibited undying patriotism. Any questions?" All three men shook their heads. "He was dispensed to a black op division in Vietnam and succeeded at every mission he was assigned. His reputation as a fierce, cagy soldier grew, as did the importance of his missions. He had over 300 confirmed kills in Vietnam, although the actual figure was probably closer to 1000. Wilson not only had the respect of his commanding officers, but the respect of the men who followed him into battle, due to his motto of 'everyone in, everyone out - no exceptions.' He did lose soldiers under his command on several occasions, but he always brought their bodies back. He never had one MIA." Beuhler stopped at the sound of the Presidents buzzer. Burke quickly answered it and gave his secretary strict orders that he was not to be disturbed. "I believe it was 1971 when he saved a platoon of soldiers from an ambush. By that time he had already received three Silver Stars, a couple Purple Hearts, and just about every other medal the armed services had to offer; but saving the platoon got him the big one, he was awarded the Congressional Medal of Honor. He stayed in Vietnam until the end and here is where the story gets a little personal.

In 1975, before we pulled out, I was assigned to head up a trade negotiation team by President Ford to discuss commerce with the North Vietnamese. Washington knew we were done in Vietnam and I was there to establish a black market. Needless to say, the plan back-fired; I'm sure you've seen pictures of the famous helicopter siege on our embassy. My team and I were arrested and tortured. The North Vietnamese were convinced our actions were not, let's say, honorable. I had no real information to give our captors, so they executed one member of my four man staff each day. On the fifth day, the day I was sure to be executed, a lieutenant colonial Green Beret rescued me from certain death. He was phenomenal. I estimate he took out 45 North Vietnamese during my rescue mission. He located the bodies of my men, loaded them with us in a truck, and drove 14 hours back through North Vietnam where we were airlifted by special forces to a naval carrier. Suffice to say, I put a lot of pressure on the lieutenant colonial's commanding officer to recommend him for another medal of honor, which he received on Christmas Eve, 1975." A little shaken from the story, Beuhler thanked Grady for the glass of water he set in front of him. "He was the most highly decorated soldier of the Vietnam War, or any war for that matter. He conducted special op training in North Carolina for the next year and then, in January of 1977, was assigned a top-secret black op back in Vietnam. He located and infiltrated concealed North Vietnamese POW camps and retrieved six of our soldiers. Two of them died before they got out, but Wilson brought their remains back home for an honorable burial. He received a third Congressional Medal of Honor from President Carter, but could never wear the patch on his uniform since the mission never existed. Everyone in the loop knew who Wilson was; to put it in perspective, he made Rambo look like a pussy." Sullivan interrupted Beuhler's reminiscing,

"This is all very informative Mr. Beuhler, but what does it have to do with the problem at hand?" Beuhler looked at President Burke.

"Let Mr. Beuhler finish, Tom."

"After that mission Wilson was proselyted by the CIA, he was a full bird colonial and perfect for their needs. The CIA staged Wilson's death and opened a seven digit account in a Swiss bank; thus, the beginning of Brown's wealth. Wilson was given the code name 'Galahad,' the bravest knight of the round table."

"I heard that name 15 years ago during some Congressional meetings involving the CIA and NSA, he was our top spook," President Burke injected.

"Oh, he was much more than that. During his service in the CIA from 1978 to 1992, he caused more havoc throughout the world than you care to know about. In those days of international terrorists for hire, Carlos the Jackal was the biggest threat to the United States. Even though Carlos was getting up in years, he was still a venerable adversary. The CIA gave Galahad the responsibility of making him a non-threat. Galahad was the perfect spook, he could use guerilla warfare, or James Bond charm, and was a master of disguise, similar to Carlos himself. But Galahad's M.O. was entirely different - the Jackal created a network of priests and poor people to hide his identity, Galahad simply killed anyone who got close to him. He tracked Carlos down and, legend has it, the fight of the century ensued, with Galahad beating him within an inch of his life. He told Carlos he found him once and he could find him again. As he left, Galahad reminded the Jackal he would be looking over his shoulder every day for the rest of his life. Carlos was only a shell of himself after that and was never considered a threat in the intelligence community again." Beuhler stopped and took a sip of water.

"In 1982 I was appointed Senior Director of the NSA, the following year Galahad broke into Langley and destroyed all records connecting him to Wilson, only a faded photograph of his Vietnam days remains. It took me six months, but after a little cloak and dagger work on my own I located Galahad and met with him at a New York City deli. He was disguised as an elderly black man, and only the stare behind the brown contact lenses covering his eyes convinced me it was the same man who saved my life." Beuhler laughed, "We let the French have Carlos, even though Galahad did not approve of that decision. He had lost his sense of undying patriotism and was much more cynical than I remembered, but I guess a life of killing people will do that to one's soul. I succeeded in recruiting him, lured with the promise of large sums of money. Galahad foresaw the cold war in the 80's and knew a lot of high-ranking politicians and their friends would make a killing. He did whatever the government needed to have done over the next several years, from El Salvador, to Iran, to Israel, and we paid him well. His biggest contribution to the nation was the part he played in overthrowing Gorbachev and installing democracy in Russia. It was Galahad who held Gorbachev hostage while Yeltsin took control. We paid him over $300 million for that mission, and in hindsight, it was a small price to pay for the end of the cold war." Grady asked permission to ask a question.

"So why all the hard feelings if Brown's a national hero?"

"Very good, young man, you are a smart one," Beuhler said, smiling at Grady.

"At the end of 1992, right before President Burke took office, Galahad realized his days as a spook were numbered. The government was only using him sparingly in the Gulf War and the order he expected to kill Hussein never came. In December of 1992 there were break-ins at the NSA, FBI and CIA, top-secret computer discs were stolen along with some other very incriminating documents. I met with Galahad in Raleigh, North Carolina on Christmas Day and he showed me copies of the evidence he had, very, very damaging evidence against the United States government. He could directly link half of Congress to kickbacks and put us in a lousy position in the new world order with our best allies, including Israel, Saudi Arabia and England."

"So what happened?" the President asked.

"I asked him what he wanted for his silence. I knew we could never have him terminated because if we were lucky enough to kill him, his death would set off his insurance policy to make sure all the evidence was given directly to the media and foreign governments. He said all he wanted was his life back. I pulled a few strings, transferred $750 million into a trust, and gave him the same status as someone in the witness protection program. That explains why Roger Brown's life starts in 1992. So gentlemen, up until now both sides lived up to their end of the bargain. Galahad called me early this morning and asked me to use whatever influence I had to help save his daughter."

"What does he want?" Sullivan asked.

"First, he wants the White House to keep former Vice President Day in line about the cover story," Beuhler stated.

"That's understandable," the President said, "I can do that."

"Second, he wants an FBI agent named Taylor to be the only person involved with this case. For some reason he trusts this Taylor man, knowing Galahad it's probably out of necessity," Beuhler said.

"Ellis, make contact with this Agent Taylor and give him whatever he needs. Keep everyone else in the dark and report directly to me on this matter," Burke commanded.

"Yes, sir," Ellis responded.

"I believe if we cooperate and help Brown get his daughter back, the status quo will go on," Beuhler finished. Chief of Staff Sullivan, feeling left out of the loop, barked,

"Why not let the evidence he has come out in the open and let the chips fall where they may? Why are we giving in to his demands?" The President began to answer but was cut off by Beuhler.

"Oh, Mr. Sullivan, don't be so naive. It would do the country much harm, I assure you. And I think we are missing the point - a little girl has been kidnaped and, even though it's not the grandchild of a dignitary, I feel we should do what we can to save her life." Sullivan tried to interrupt, but Beuhler continued. "And if it was my grandchild who had been kidnaped, I would not call the police or the FBI, I would call Galahad - he's the best person for the job and he knows it. And finally, sir, if it ever got out of this room that you were opposed to helping Galahad rescue his daughter, I assure you he would kill you, your wife, and your children."

7

The lack of sleep and the amphetamines had Roger's mind racing at light speed. He realized there was a distinct possibility that he could be ahead of the kidnappers and decided to retrace the last 20 miles he traveled. He thought and re-thought every possibility imaginable, verbalizing his impressions to himself. While heading north, back toward Austin, he concluded, 'Probably 72 hours, that's normal time. I must find out who, or what, they want for ransom.' Roger hypothesized that the kidnappers wanted the job completed, from the hit to the pay off, within 72 hours. 'They probably changed vehicles at some point, maybe a car within a truck. Don't look for vehicles, look for characteristics of the kidnappers.' He made a mental note to share his suspicions with Taylor when he spoke with him. He knew he caught a break with Peggy Short's electronic diary, now he had to capitalize on it.

The odometer indicated Roger had backtracked 19.7 miles since stopping at the Fed-Ex office and the puke and choke. He had entered the restroom of the fast food restaurant as a bald FBI agent and exited ten minutes later as a man in his mid 50's with a slightly receding hairline. Disguised as a Tupperware salesman, a lost tourist, or prospective buyer of real estate, he stealthily investigated every flea bag hotel. The scam was always the same, first, avoid bringing any attention to himself, second, ask the clerk behind the desk (or the cleaning lady) if he or she saw anyone that fit the description of the characters in Ms. Short's chronicles.

"Excuse me ma'am," Roger said, to the clerk behind the desk. This was his 14th stop and would be his last until he spoke with Taylor. The clock above the pretty young Mexican girl read 12:12 p.m. He realized it had been one full day since the whole affair began and he lost himself for a moment.

"Sir? Sir? Are you okay?" Roger caught his equilibrium.

"Nothing that a glass of water won't fix," he responded, using his best Texas accent. The young lady presented Roger with a glass of water from the cooler behind the desk.

"Are you okay, sir?"

"Yes ma'am," Roger answered. "My name is T.S. Strong. I'm the president of Strong Holding Company. Have you ever heard of me?" The young girl shook her head.

"Sorry, sir, no."

"Well, anyway, I sent two teams of analysts down to these parts. You see I'm from the Big D, Dallas, you know." The young girl nodded, amused by the old man. "Well, anyway, I was supposed to meet with my analysts around noon today, and to be honest with you young lady, I don't know if it was at this hotel or the one 15 miles down the road toward San Antonio." Wanting to help the funny old man, the young girl asked,

"What's their name? I'll check the computer."

"Well, you see ma'am, that's the funny thing. Because of the nature of our business, my associates may be traveling under an assumed name."

"Why?" the clerk asked. Roger cautiously looked around and leaned over the counter.

"You see ma'am, if the people that we buy the real estate from know that we're interested, they kick up the price of the land," he whispered, in a low voice. Roger's explanation worked like a charm.

"What do your associates look like?" the clerk questioned.

"Well ma'am, there would be five men, and oh yeah, a woman," Roger paused and winked at the young girl. "One of the fellows likes to bring his sweetheart along with him on the overnight trips, they may have even brought their little girl with them."

"I don't remember a party of six. I've been here since 8:00 p.m. last night, you know, pulling a double."

"Yes, yes, I understand." Roger decided to take one last crack at the pretty young lady. "You see, ma'am, because of the nature of our business, they might have split up. My associates are. . . how can I say this, a little peculiar. Two of the men are of Spanish heritage, one is from Arabia and two are American boys. The woman is also Spanish and the little girl, oh, let me think, she must be four or five by now." The phone rang as Roger finished and the clerk transferred the caller to one of the rooms.

"Sorry, I can't help you," the clerk said.

"Well, thank you for your time and the glass of water." Roger donned his hat and headed for the door.

"Oh, sir?" the clerk called, as he turned the knob to leave.

"Yes, ma'am?" Roger answered.

"I don't know if this will help you find your business associates, but two men, an American and I don't know what the other was, checked in around midnight." Roger removed his hat and methodically walked back toward the desk. "I thought they were gay," she said, half laughing. Roger forced a laugh and concentrated on suppressing the urge to jump over the counter and beat the next line out of her.

"Go on, sweetheart."

"A tan van picked them up this morning at," she stopped and looked at the check out sheet, "8:51 a.m." Rogers instincts began to tingle. "They left the car they came in in the parking lot, if they don't come back for it in 24 hours we have to call the police and have it towed."

"Which way was the van headed, ma'am?"

"They made a left out of the parking lot, the only thing down that road is the westbound entrance to the interstate."

"Yep, that would be right, checking out the grove real estate," Roger drawled. "I guess we had a problem with miscommunication. Where's the car? I'll let you know if it's theirs and save you the trouble of having to contact the police." The clerk checked the registration and informed Roger it was a dark green Honda Accord with Colorado plates. Roger thanked the pretty Mexican girl and told her he would let her know if the car belonged to one of his associates.

Roger drove his Caddy to the parking lot behind the hotel and found the Accord in less than a minute. The dashboard clock read 12:41 p.m. He wanted to call FBI Agent Taylor as soon as possible. Roger picked the door lock in seconds and was immediately confronted with the fetor of marijuana and cheap cologne. The car was registered to the same man who checked into the hotel, John Smith of Denver, Colorado. Roger did not find the smoking gun he was looking for and hopped out to check the trunk. He spotted a small stain on the carpet and partially shut the trunk lid to get a point of reference from the stain. Roger inspected the area closely and discovered a few fine hairs stuck to the metal. He went to the Caddy and retrieved a pair of tweezers, a magnifying glass and a sheet of white paper. After carefully pulling the hairs from the underside of the trunk, Roger inspected them under the glass against the white paper. They were unquestionably human, and he thought the color was close to Tris'. Roger's mind was racing as he closed the trunk and doors to the Honda. If this was one of the kidnappers cars, it was the one that had Tris in it, not the one they intended the FBI to find. They were too far away from San Antonio to give the impression of running the Mexican border. Roger's instincts told him the kidnappers initially split into three different groups, and two of them just reunited. The third faction would probably join up after ditching the get away vehicle closer to the border.

Roger started the Caddy and headed for the entrance to the interstate, he knew he was about four hours behind them, but still kept an eye open for a tan van. It was 1:11 p.m. He wanted to call Taylor and change back into FBI Agent, Coyle. If he did have casual contact with the kidnappers, and Tris was with them, the last thing he needed was for her to cry, 'oh, daddy!' He dialed the private line to his office at the ranch, which in turn dialed Agent Taylor at the FBI. Taylor answered on the third ring,

"FBI, Taylor."

"Were you assigned the case?" Roger asked. Taylor connected the voice to the man with the glare in his eyes at the library.

"You must have some connections," Taylor answered.

"I imagine they want you to give them hourly updates," Roger stated.

"Something like that," Taylor replied.

"Be smart, tell them what they want to hear, but nothing specific. You know the drill, some good developments, etc.," Roger ordered.

"I understand," Taylor replied. "Where are you?"

"Don't worry about that, I have it taken care of."

"Really? How's that?" Taylor inquired.

"You'll be getting a Fed Ex package containing the names and descriptions of who I presume the kidnappers are. Have your new D.C. friends run them through the CIA, NSA, and Interpol. I gather you can run them through the Bureau yourself," Roger said, ignoring Taylor's questions.

"How come I don't believe the trace on this call? It's showing your ranch."

"Taylor, stop playing fucking kid games! This is the fucking major league!" Roger said in the cold voice of Galahad. "Be smart in what you tell the people in D.C. Give them the impression that things are moving along well, but don't let the left hand know what the right hand is doing."

"Okay, okay, it's your ball game, we'll play it your way," Taylor responded, shaken by Roger's tone and intensity.

"I'll contact you in about six hours to find out what you've come up with. And remember, it's my daughter's life, no fucking games." Roger clicked off the phone before Taylor had an opportunity to respond.

The effects of the amphetamines were wearing off. Roger wanted to change back into FBI Agent, Coyle as soon as possible and he needed sleep. He pulled into the first motel he saw and, after paying the $39.95 plus tax, left instructions for a wake-up call in exactly four hours. He flipped the desk clerk a twenty to insure the call was made. Roger entered the room and immediately went to the bathroom and transformed himself into

Agent Coyle. He would head west on the interstate and call Taylor to explain the homing device in the Fed-Ex package, and see what he developed on the leads, when he awoke. Roger set a travel alarm clock for 6:30 p.m. (four hours and ten minutes later), laid his head on the pillows, and was asleep in seconds.

8

The receptionist arrived at Taylor's office seconds after he hung up with Brown. She placed a Federal Express package on his desk and advised him it had already been cleared through security. He removed a manilla envelope from the box and briefly examined the homing device. The envelope contained a list of Roger's suspects, including a general description of each and known aliases. Taylor dialed his new best friend in Washington.

"Grady." Taylor was relieved the number he was given was a direct line to the Assistant Chief of Staff. When they first spoke a few hours ago, Grady had followed the bureaucratic protocol to the letter. Taylor's immediate supervisor called to inform him that the Undersecretary of the FBI would be calling him to advise him the Assistant Chief of Staff would be calling him to discuss the kidnaping of former Vice President Day's daughter. It reminded Taylor of the old joke, 'how many Congressmen does it take to screw in a light bulb?' The Undersecretary of the FBI made it quite clear that Taylor was to give the White House all the assistance he could. Grady made it quite clear that the White House wanted Taylor, and Taylor alone, to handle the case. He ended their conversation with a subtle threat, "you report everything, and I mean everything, back through me and we'll get along just fine." Taylor took him seriously, he had no desire to be the first FBI agent stationed permanently in Anchorage.

"Taylor, here."

"Some developments, I hope," Grady prompted.

"Yes sir, along with some requests."

"Developments first," Grady ordered.

"I had contact with Brown. He sent a Fed Ex package to me requesting we check out some possible suspects," Taylor said.

"How do you know it's from Brown?" Grady asked.

"He called me before the package arrived," Taylor responded.

"You traced the call?" Grady asked.

"Yes sir, to his ranch."

"Odd, don't you think?"

"Sir, I'm still in the blind here. I'm just doing what I'm told. He also sent some type of state-of-the-art homing device," Taylor added.

"What's that about?" Grady questioned.

"I don't know. The tech boys tell me it's only one-way," Taylor answered.

"Meaning?" Grady asked.

"He can turn the beacon off and on. They also said it has a range of 1500 miles," Taylor stated.

"What do you take from that?" Grady asked.

"He'll only call in the calvary when he needs it."

"Yes, I see." Grady said. "Anything else to report, other than you need some information?"

"No, sir. We're finishing up our interviews and should have a report in a couple hours," Taylor said, as he picked the FBI interview report out of his bin. "Brown said he would call back around 8:00 p.m. tonight to see if we came up with anything."

"Okay. What does Brown need?"

"He needs the CIA, NSA, and Interpol, as he put it, to check on some suspects," Taylor said. "I'll take care of the FBI search."

"Shoot," Grady said.

"The first is a man in his late 50's, of Spanish descent, who is using the alias Don Juan. Brown presupposes he may be Wilfred Benito Sanchez." Taylor stopped to make sure Grady was getting everything.

"Go on," Grady said.

"The second is an Arab, probably Iranian, under the alias of Kabiv. The third is another Spaniard named Jesus. Number four, an American, alias George. Number five, also American, alias Eric. Brown indicated this Eric may be a pilot. The last is a Hispanic female, alias Illiana." Taylor decided not to give any more information to the Assistant Chief of Staff.

"You keep me up to date on every little development on this case," Grady warned. "Check out his ranch and let me know about the FBI interviews ASAP." Grady hung up the phone. Taylor concluded he did not like this Grady guy. He decided he would try to help Brown get his daughter back and just tell Grady what he wanted to hear. Taylor gathered the interview file and headed to lunch. On his way out he instructed one of the younger, less experienced agents to follow the trace on Brown's house and start the process of requesting a search warrant for the ranch. Taylor knew it would take at least a week before a judge would grant a warrant.

"On what grounds?" the young agent asked.

"Go to law and have them research it," Taylor said, giving himself plausible deniability, but still following Grady's instructions. Grady made the necessary phone calls to the CIA, NSA, and Interpol. After completing the last request he dialed the intercom to the President's personal secretary.

"Yes, Ellis, what can I do for you?" She was a black lady in her mid-forties who, like many of the staff, came to D.C. with the President and was very loyal to the Commander and Chief.

"I was wondering if #1 could spare me a few moments later today." Ellis said, politely.

"If you are referring to The President of the United States, he left strict instructions to fit you in as soon as possible if you called." She hated how the staff picked up the Secret Service's code names. She felt he should be referred to as the President, or at least as Mr. Burke, not a number. "The President will have ten minutes to spare at 7:30 p.m. before attending a dinner," she stated.

"That would be fine, thank you." Grady crossed his fingers that he would have a response from the other agencies by then. Chief of Staff, Thomas Sullivan overheard the secretary's conversation and made a mental note to be in the Oval Office at 7:30 p.m.

Grady grabbed a Snickers bar out of his desk and placed a call to Anthony Bucco, Agent Taylor's Station Chief. When Grady first spoke to Bucco about the White House wanting Taylor, and Taylor alone, to handle the kidnaping of former VP Day's granddaughter, they decided the Station Chief should run a parallel investigation. Bucco was indebted to Grady for a favor he did for him three years ago. After a series of bank robberies in the mid-west, Bucco received invaluable information from Grady's contacts at the Treasury Department that helped him solve the case. Grady highlighted Bucco and arranged for him to receive an accommodation and promotion to Station Chief. In his little world of Assistant Chief of Staff, Grady was a master at empire building. He was not as influential as his idol, Charles Beuhler, but Grady had a lot of contacts where the tire hit the road.

Coming from the unlikely city of Las Vegas, Ellis Elvis Grady was the product of a broken home. His mother, a personnel manager for a small casino, did her best to raise him by the Good Book after his father disappeared before Ellis' fourth birthday. Being smaller than other kids his age, Ellis quickly learned the power of words and the importance of keeping his enemies closest. He missed the Vietnam draft by six months and attended Nevada State University on a partial scholarship. The myriad of jobs he held during his college years earned him a degree in moxie, which turned out to be more instrumental than his degrees in history and criminal justice. After graduation, Ellis worked for a public relations firm outside of Vegas for a year before accepting a job in advertising and relocating to Kansas City. He became involved in a campaign for a farmer who was running for the United States Congress. The farmer lost, but Ellis caught the political bug. After working on several Senate campaigns, Ellis aligned himself with Burke's presidential crusade. In less than six months he was the #3 man on the campaign. Burke was victorious and rewarded the hard-working, fast-thinking kid from Nevada with a position in the National Security Agency. Grady was pleased with his accomplishments in the political arena. Working at the NSA had its perks; good restaurant reservations, tickets to sporting events, etc., but it was the power of the Presidency that turned his motor. Ellis used his intellect and his moxie to weave through the political maze of the inner loop, eventually attaining the #2 position on the President's staff.

The CIA, NSA, and Interpol reported back to the Assistant Chief of Staff shortly after 7:00 p.m. Grady prepared a file for his meeting with #1 at 7:30 p.m. He was pleased Station Chief, Bucco confirmed that Taylor reported everything they had on the case. He was a little curious why Taylor did not discuss the FBI interviews with him, but accepted Bucco's explanation that he probably wanted to review the file before going into detail about it with the White House. Grady was also happy to hear that Taylor followed his instructions to trace Brown's phone. What neither Bucco, nor Taylor knew, was that it was simply a test for Taylor; Brown's call meant nothing, but Grady was pleased to see his orders were being carried out to the letter.

The Assistant Chief of Staff entered the Oval Office to find President Burke in his formal wear having a drink with his boss, Chief of Staff, Tom Sullivan. Grady was momentarily taken back at the sight of Sullivan, but recomposed himself by intentionally dropping some papers.

"Mr. President, Mr. Sullivan." Grady addressed both men as he stooped to pick the papers up off the floor.

"Ellis, bring me up to speed quickly, I have a dinner to attend," the President said, taking a seat behind his desk. "I called former Vice President Day and the old bastard reluctantly agreed to play along. He promised he would keep his granddaughter out of sight and lay low for a few more days."

"Very good, sir," Grady replied. "Agent Taylor, the one Brown, a.k.a. Galahad, wanted to deal with exclusively, contacted me today after receiving a call from him," Grady stated.

"What did he want?" Sullivan asked.

"He asked that we use the CIA, NSA, and Interpol to run checks on six people." Grady directed his response directly to the President.

"And?" the President asked.

"Galahad is good. He's very good. We were unable to locate a record on two of the individuals, but the other four could very well be possible suspects in the kidnaping."

"Who are they?" the President asked, motioning for Grady to speed up. Grady quickly ran through the list.

"During their investigation, the FBI found a library employee named Margaret Short executed in her apartment. They also located a passenger van that fits eyewitness descriptions of the vehicle the kidnapers fled from the library in."

"What do you derive from all this?" The President asked.

"The woman who was murdered was probably involved with one of the kidnappers and Galahad probably already knew about it," Grady answered.

"Do you think he killed her?" President Burke asked.

"No sir. The preliminary autopsy report indicated she was already dead 48 hours."

"So you think the kidnappers are probably somewhere around San Antonio? Or in Mexico by now?" Sullivan asked.

"I don't know, sir. The FBI said their trail was headed for Mexico, but they could not make a positive confirmation." The President sat back in thought for a few minutes.

"It makes sense. The kidnappers demanded the release of three terrorists. If memory serves me right, Day chaired a committee that promoted the imprisonment of terrorists who committed crimes against the United States," the President said.

"Should I pass that information on to Taylor to give to Galahad?" Grady asked.

"Hell, yes, boy!" The President yelled, as he rose from his chair. "Give this Galahad everything he needs to get his daughter back. The more I thought about what Charles Beuhler said about Galahad, the more that came back to me. I recall that during the Congressional hearings held a few years back, every time Galahad's name was mentioned, or about to be mentioned, we went into private chambers. This Galahad was not only the best, he was a mean motherfucker."

It was almost 8:00 p.m. when the meeting with President Burke ended. Grady literally ran back to his office to call Taylor to let him know the transmission was on its way. He received confirmation that the fax completed at 7:57 p.m. Relieved that he handed off the information, Grady decided to call it a day and treat himself to a real dinner. As he was tying up a few loose ends, Chief of Staff, Sullivan appeared in his doorway.

"Yes sir?" Grady said. Sullivan entered the room, shut the door behind him, and walked to Grady's desk. Impeccably dressed in a $2500 suit, Chief of Staff, Thomas Brian Sullivan was a tall, distinguished looking man with gray hair and capped teeth. He was not a man to tangle with in the White House inner circle. Raised in the blue-blood section outside of Boston, Sullivan graduated from Yale and became a behind the scenes politician even before he passed the bar. He caught a rising star from Pennsylvania a decade into his career, but his aspirations of being on the tail of the comet were extinguished when the Presidential hopeful was killed in a plane crash. Sullivan switched houses, philosophically and politically, and recognized Burke's potential at the New Hampshire primary. He joined Burke's cause and, at the recommendation of the party, became Burke's campaign manager after the convention. Although the two men worked well together, Sullivan always felt a little on the outs with #1 because he was the party's choice, not Burke's. Reciprocally, Burke had the taste of sour milk in his mouth from having to honor the favor.

Sullivan leaned intimidatingly over his assistant and spoke in a low voice.

"The next time you set up a meeting with #1 without confirming with me, will be the last day you work in this administration."

"But, sir, the Presi. . ." Still leaning imposingly over Grady's desk, Sullivan cut him off,

"Who the fuck hired you? Everything you do with this situation you run by me first. Anything you even think of doing with this situation you run by me first. Then we'll give #1 the run down."

"Yes, sir," Grady said, more angry than scared. He knew what Sullivan was doing, and if he were in Sullivan's place he would probably do the same thing; but that didn't mean he had to like it. "I apologize if I got out of line. Just the enthusiasm of a man who lives for his job." Sullivan knew Grady was a workaholic and took him at his word.

9

What was that sound? The phone was ringing. Was it the phone? Cat, get the phone, it's ringing and ringing. Roger picked up the receiver only to hear the sound of elevator music. He glanced at the travel alarm next to the phone, but couldn't focus on its glow in the dark face. Who was calling? Where am I? The phone slipped from Roger's hand and the twilight world of fuzz and confusion ebbed to slumber. 'I'm so tired,' he said, as he fell back to the comfort of the warm pillow and cool sheets. The loud, ringing buzz of the travel alarm scared Roger into an upright position. The events of the past 24 hours slowly returned to him. The face of the annoying travel alarm read 6:40 p.m. Roger took a quick shower and adjusted the mustache of FBI Agent Coyle. He picked up a map of Texas in the lobby and checked out of the $39.95 plus tax motel.

While sitting in the diner adjacent to the motel, Roger formulated a plan. Using the place mat as a straight edge, he drew a line on the map from San Antonio to Boulder. He then drew a second line from the hotel, where he located the Honda, to Boulder. The point where the lines intersected was a town in the Texas panhandle called Dalhart. Roger thought it was as good a place as any to begin to look for the kidnappers to regroup. The idea to keep the plan simple, from the kidnappers point of view, gave the mid-size city of Dalhart more credence than he originally thought. Roger finished the lasagna special, paid the bill, and started the 500 mile trip to Dalhart. He drove the Caddy 31 miles east and picked up the interstate north. It was 8:08 p.m. when he reached the on ramp and darkness was beginning to veil the Indian summer night. He knew he had the advantage of traveling faster than the kidnappers, especially with the cover of FBI Agent Coyle. Roger was confident that if Dalhart was the rendezvous location, he would be in the city before the kidnappers arrived. He knew it was time to take Agent Taylor into his complete confidence, he had no choice. Traveling at close to 100 mph, a fleeting thought occurred to him; what would he do if a State Trooper did stop him and did not buy the FBI cover? Roger knew the answer, he would have to kill him. There was no middle ground, but perhaps Taylor could help. He dialed his private office, which in return dialed Taylor's office.

"FBI, Taylor."

"Did you get what I need?" Roger asked. This time Taylor immediately recognized the voice.

"Yes, I think it's going to be a big help."

"The ransom note, how long did the kidnappers give to meet their demands?"

"72 hours, just as you said," Taylor replied.

"And what exactly do they want?" Roger asked.

"They want the release of three convicted terrorists, two Iranian, one Libyan. The Libyan was connected to the World Trade Center bombing. The other two were convicted countermining a ploy to bomb a shopping mall, they were apprehended before their plan came to fruition," Taylor answered.

"How do they want it done?" Roger asked.

"A military plane to Spain and then a commercial flight to Libya."

"Okay, listen, tell your friends in D.C. to go along with the plan. Have the prisoners transferred from their cells to McGuire, but don't let them board the jet. Just give the impression that we are going along with their demands," Roger stated. "Do not let them get out of the country under any circumstances."

"Okay, I'll pass it on," Taylor said.

"The kidnappers probably have moles on the inside, like the Short lady; so playing along is the name of the game." Roger knew this was the moment of truth, he waited for Taylor's reaction to his comment on Peggy Short.

"Shit, I'm in way over my head," Taylor said.

"Hang in there and trust me as I trust you. Right now I trust you more than any other person on the face of this earth," Roger said, knowing Taylor bit, but needed to be reeled in very carefully.

"The D.C. fellows mandate that I keep them informed on everything," Taylor said. Roger had a brainstorm.

"That's okay, you tell them the truth." Roger realized feeding Taylor misinformation would keep the others out of his hair. "Do you understand?" Roger asked. Taylor caught on.

"I understand completely," Taylor replied.

"You know what that device I sent you is for?" Roger asked.

"The calvary," Taylor said.

"Exactly. What type of response can I count on?" Roger asked.

"Less than one hour," Taylor responded.

"Now tell me about Wilfred Benito Sanchez," Roger demanded.

"He is considered one of the most feared terrorists by the intelligence community. His other alias, the one he is better known by, is Bambino de Jackal, or. . ."

"Baby of the Jackal," Roger finished, cutting Taylor off. "I got lucky, the age and M.O. fit."

"Be careful Brown, it's noted that he was the most loyal disciple of Carlos the Jackal. Do you know who Carlos the Jackal is?" Galahad smiled as he continued his drive north on the interstate, the speedometer reaching 110 mph.

"Who do you think put Carlos the Jackal out of commission?" Once again, Taylor was silent. "Did you ever hear of a spook named Galahad?"

"Sure, I always assumed Galahad was a myth of the CIA," Taylor answered.

"I assure you I am no myth," Roger laughed.

"Oh, Christ! Why me! I didn't ask for this assignment!"

"Just ask your D.C. friends what 'everyone in, everyone out' means, then you'll have a better understanding. Please, trust me."

"What choice do I have!" Taylor exclaimed.

"I know Sanchez and his side kick Jesus, or whatever he calls himself these days, better than they do. They'll keep a low profile, keep their plan simple, and use disguises to maintain their anonymity. Tell me about the girl, Illiana."

"We believe Illiana is Consuela Marquez of El Salvador. Part prostitute and part sociopath, her M.O. is to fuck her marks to death, literally," Taylor announced.

"That's good to know. How about the Iranian, Kabiv?" Roger inquired.

"Nothing, absolutely nothing," Taylor said.

"The two Americans?" Roger asked.

"Nothing on George yet, but we think Eric is Eric Long, a former F-15 pilot who was tossed out of the military for attitude problems. He also has a sheet for air drug trafficking," Taylor said.

"What does he look like?" Roger asked.

"Around 5'10", 165 pounds, light brown hair, he reminds you of the movie star Brad Pitt, but more rugged."

"I gather the former VP was persuaded to play along," Roger said.

"That's the word I get."

"Taylor, I'm traveling under an alias as an FBI agent. I need to know that if I get into a jam, say a local cop or a State Trooper, you'll back me up," Roger said, being careful not to disclose his assumed name.

"Gotcha covered. They even brought a cot into my office so I'm at your disposal 24 hours a day," Taylor answered.

"I'm a little past San Antonio, did they find the get away car yet?"

"Oh shit, I forgot! They found a passenger van that matched the description of an eyewitness at the crime scene on the outskirts of San Antonio," Taylor said.

"Good," Roger responded, knowing Taylor would pass on the wrong information to his new friends in D.C. "Taylor, one last thing, please check on my wife."

"I already did, she's coming along fine."

"Thanks. I'll be talking to you."

10

Chief of Staff, Sullivan relaxed in the whirlpool of the exclusive men's club located on the outskirts of the nation's capital. The $46,000 annual membership fee kept the local riff-raff out. Of course, Sullivan did not pay the membership fee, that came as a perk; not from the United States government, but from John Kelley, a lobbyist from Jamaica who Sullivan dealt with for many years. Kelley, British born and raised, was in some ways an assassin himself - he was a lobbyist who catered to the highest bidder. The Chief of Staff had a manifold of dealings with the English Jamaican, always in the area of inside information, e.g. defense contracts and company bids. Kelley brokered the information to interested parties for a handsome profit. His payment to Sullivan was never monetary, or traceable. The use of the health club as Kelley's guest, his $2.1 million dollar home purchased from an estate for a mere $500,000, the scholarships his three children received to Ivy League schools, etc. The arrangement was symbiotic.

Sullivan exited the whirlpool in the locker room and dried off. He sat on the bench and sighed, relieved that #1 did not require him to attend another boring state function that night. The clock on the wall showed 9:54 p.m. and Sullivan's thoughts began to retreat from those surrounding the White House. As Sullivan sat reflecting, a man in his early 20's, wrapped in a towel, entered the locker room and approached him. He was close to six feet tall, with the slender body of a swimmer, and appeared to be of Italian or Spanish decent, with dark brown hair and brown eyes. The young man cracked a little smile of

acknowledgment and knelt down in front of the Chief of Staff.
He slowly ran his hands up Sullivan's legs, moving his towel
aside to kiss the top of his thighs, as the Chief of Staff leaned
back against the wall and spread his legs. The dark haired man
moved closer and rhythmically kissed and licked his penis while
the Chief of Staff stroked the back of his neck for
encouragement. After several minutes, Sullivan gently lifted the
young man's head and guided him with his eyes. The man stood
up and let the Chief of Staff fondle him, he knew the routine.
Sullivan enjoyed feeling the soft skin of another man's penis
tighten over its shaft as it became erect in his hands. Sullivan
guided him again with his eyes and the young man stepped over
the bench and leaned spread eagle against the wall. Sullivan
stroked himself with his left hand to ensure a good erection,
while he wet his fingers and rubbed them over the young man's
anus. The Chief of Staff positioned himself behind the young
man and slowly entered him, letting out a sigh of pleasure. The
young man responded by thrusting backward against Sullivan's
penis as he entered and exited his rectum. The Chief of Staff let
out a primal scream as he came deep inside the young boy and
bit him on the back. The young concubine silently turned,
cleaned Sullivan's penis, and vanished.

After a long, hot shower, Sullivan returned to the locker area
to dress. Sitting on the bench under a 'no smoking' sign,
smoking a cigarette, was John Brian Kelley. He was impeccably
dressed in a dark blue, silk suit with a white shirt and light blue
ascot. Kelley was in his early forties and had a receding hairline
that shimmered when the light hit it. Kelley was educated in a
finishing school outside of the London city limits and carried
himself with an air of chicness. The man with the Irish sounding
name was the only child of an affluent British family that did
very well for a period in reinsurance, but went bankrupt in the
mid sixties. His father met his maker at the end of a rope and his
mother was institutionalized shortly thereafter. Armed only with
his snobbish charm, Kelley found it easy and profitable to deal in
the information of the wealthy. The culmination of a life of
selling secrets was a twelve bedroom house on the island of
Jamaica. Money begets power and Kelley soon worked his way

up the jet-set food chain, becoming a reliable source of dirt for the highest bidder.

"Hello, old chap'" Kelley said, cheerfully.

"Hello, John," Sullivan answered.

"What's doing these days?"

"Same old, same old," Sullivan responded, assuming Kelley wanted some information.

"I need your help in a little matter," Kelley stated.

"What's that?" Sullivan questioned.

"Oh, the kidnaping of Day's grandchild."

"Why would a top player like you be concerned with the Day kidnaping?"

"Oh, for a client."

"No can do on this one old friend," Sullivan said, as he put on his trousers.

"Did I mention it was for a very special client?" Kelley tried.

"I don't give a damn who it's for. Letting you know Boeing is getting a big defense contract a few hours before the news hits the street so you and your friends can make a killing in the stock market is one thing; but this, no can do." Kelley was silent while Sullivan finished dressing. As he headed for the door behind Kelley he noticed a handful of photographs on the bench beside him. The pictures showed the Chief of Staff having homosexual sex, in the most explicit manner, with several different young men.

"Sorry old chap. Hated to have to do this, but tomorrow morning at 9:30 a.m. I've got to give this very important man something - it's either going to be these photos or something they want to know about the Day kidnaping. Let's just say these clients play hard ball." Sullivan knew the risk of the game he played and presumed that one day it would come to this; not necessarily his sexual preference, but something inevitably creeps up and bites you in the ass when you walk the line.

"What do you want to know?" Sullivan asked.

"My clients are not sure, they know the FBI is sending up a lot of fodder, but no real investigation. They would be very grateful for whatever light you could shed on the situation,"

Kelley replied. Sullivan hesitated, glanced down at the photos again, and then spoke.

"It's not Day's granddaughter that was kidnaped."

"Say again, old chap?"

"The kidnappers mistakenly abducted the wrong little girl," Sullivan iterated.

"Oh, my," Kelley exclaimed. "Whose little girl did they kidnap?" Sullivan knew he would be dead as a door nail if he told Kelley the true identity of the child's father.

"Some rich cattle ranchers kid named Brown, Roger Brown," Sullivan said.

"That explains a lot. These will be staying with me, old friend," Kelley said, as he gathered up the pictures.

Assistant Chief of Staff, Grady ate one forkful of the sweet and sour pork out of the white cardboard take out container when the phone rang.

"Grady," he answered.

"Taylor here, sir," the FBI agent stated. It was 9:15 p.m. on Thursday, the second full day of the kidnaping.

"Did he contact you?" Grady asked, impatiently.

"Yes, he reported he was headed for San Antonio so I arranged for some back up in the general vicinity in case the beeper goes off," Taylor said.

"Oh really?" Grady replied.

"He wanted me to ask if the people in Washington could play along with the ransom."

"What do you mean?" Grady asked, already knowing the answer.

"He thinks, as he put it, there may be moles, like the dead librarian. If we give the perception of going along with the ransom the kidnappers may fall into a false sense of security, or something. He really did not explain his reasoning." Taylor answered.

"I don't think he'll get that request. As a matter of fact, I know he will not get that request," Grady stated. "Of course I'll pass it on to the proper authorities, but the United States government does not negotiate with terrorists - even if it is perception. How did he know about Margaret Short?

"I don't know, he just mentioned it as part of the conversation," Taylor replied.

"That was not announced to the media yet. I wonder if this Mr. Brown is telling us everything," Grady asked rhetorically. "Anything else?"

"Yes," Taylor said, hesitating for a second, "Brown told me to ask the people in D.C. what the phrase 'everyone in, everyone out' means. He said it may clear up a lot of unanswered questions in my mind." Grady's heart almost stopped. He knew it was imperative to have the trust and loyalty of people in situations where they could only see one side of the coin. He chose his words carefully,

"What else did Mr. Brown tell you about himself?" Grady realized he made a tactical error handling Taylor. By emphasizing the power of the White House to cut red tape, he alienated the person holding the scissors. Grady knew he had to learn to handle people better with his words and not rely on the overwhelming power of the White House behind him.

"Some incredible credentials," Taylor said, not wanting to mention the name Galahad.

"I see," Grady said, stalling for time.

"So what does 'everyone in, everyone out' have to do with Brown?" Taylor asked, again.

"That's the motto of a three-time Congressional Medal of Honor recipient who was formerly a full bird colonial in the Green Berets and did a tour of duty with the intelligence community. That's about as far as I can go on the subject. Give me a call when Brown contacts you again." Grady hung up the phone.

Taylor was somewhat surprised that Grady, in a round about way, confirmed Brown was Galahad. The puzzle was starting to come together. Brown probably was the best person to save his daughter's life, and he probably knew where a lot of D.C.'s skeletons were buried.

11

Two hours after talking to FBI Agent, Taylor, Roger was still headed toward Dalhart. His mind had been working overtime during the uneventful drive through the Texas night. 'I wonder if Tris was the target,' he questioned aloud. The possibility that the kidnappers went after Tris to draw out Galahad intrigued him enough to ruminate the theory. 'Who?' he asked, continuing his conversation with himself. 'That could be hundreds, or even thousands. But it would have to be someone that knows my true identity, has a motive, and most importantly, has the power to carry out a plan of this size.' Roger focused on who knew his true identity. Beuhler came to mind first, he was always Roger's contact. Beuhler definitely had the influence to help in a black op, but no real power to carry it out. The man who was President at the time Roger retired was dead, so he was out of the question. The only other person who may have been able to connect Roger to Galahad was former Vice President Day, but it would have taken a lot of conjecture on his part to the hows and whys of his disappearance. All roads led him back to Beuhler. Roger continued to mull over his speculations until he saw a sign indicating Dalhart was less than 100 miles. He quickly forgot his thoughts of who may be trying to score off his past life and looked for a road heading west. Now it was time to concentrate on the task at hand, getting his daughter back.

Roger stopped at a diner just outside of the Dalhart city limits. He changed his appearance back to the good old real estate boy and ordered an early breakfast. As he handed the waitress the menu he thought of the first time he sat at Cat's station. Within minutes, the real estate broker had the three customers and two waitresses in stitches over the antics of his business associates blunders. Roger's thirty minutes of pre-dawn entertainment proved to be very informative. A Spanish man fitting the general description of Jesus had stopped in the diner only a couple hours earlier. He ordered coffee and the diner's version of an egg McMuffin and was last seen headed for Dalhart. Roger wished everyone well, left the waitress a ten dollar tip, and departed.

He began his canvas of the motels using the same M.O., but with a new occupation. Roger was a chameleon when it came to dealing with people. His intellect would size up the persons character and his instincts would guide his approach. If the desk clerk was older, he would show respect and talk of days gone by, if she was young, like the pretty Mexican girl, he would use the charm of an older uncle. He surmised Jesus, or whoever stopped in the diner for the egg McMuffin knock off, was the remaining member of the kidnapper's crew. He was probably driving to Dalhart straight from San Antonio after disposing of the get away vehicle. The town was the antithesis of a traveler's mecca and the motels were few and far between. He hit pay dirt on his fifth stop, just as the early morning sun peaked over the dusty horizon. The squalid motel was annexed to a luncheonette that had an entrance from the parking lot as well as the lobby. Roger entered the establishment to find an overweight man in his late forties, in desperate need of a bath, behind the desk. The man did not hear Roger enter, nor did he look up from the x-rated movie he was playing on a small VCR when he approached the counter.

"Howdy," Roger said.

"Need a room?" the clerk asked, without looking away from the adult film.

"Maybe," Roger responded.

"What?" the clerk answered.

"I'm looking for some business associates."

"Can't help you, mister," the clerk said. Roger laid a twenty dollar bill on the counter and the clerk looked up.

"Go ahead, take it, it's for your time." The clerk picked up the twenty and focused his attention on the wad of bills in Roger's right hand.

"What do your business associates look like?" Roger laid a fifty on the desk and went through the same spiel he used with the pretty, young Mexican girl. The clerk was thinking real hard to see if he could help his new best friend and secure more of the greenbacks.

"I don't know. . ." the clerk began. Roger laid another $50 on the desk.

"That's it until you give me something concrete."

"I'd like to help mister, but the only odd occurrence was around 4:00 a.m."

"What was that?" Roger asked.

"A Mexican man drove in the parking lot and went directly to the room of a young couple with a kid." Roger put a $100 bill on the counter, but held one end.

"Was the child a boy or a girl?"

"I believe it was a girl," the clerk said, as he felt the cowboy let go of the C note.

"The young couple, when did they check in, and what did they look like?" Roger asked, placing another hundred dollar bill on the counter under his hand. The clerk quickly checked the register.

"Mr. and Mrs. Eric Martin checked in at 7:40 p.m. last night." Roger allowed the clerk to retrieve the bills.

"What did they look like?" Roger asked, flashing three $100 bills in front of the clerk, "and what room?"

"She was Spanish, a real looker, but older than him. He was, you know, one of them pretty boys. Room 116, you can see it from here." The clerk pointed across the parking lot and Roger laid the bills on the counter. He looked into the clerks eyes and in the voice of Galahad said,

"I was never here. If I find out I was here you've watched your last smut film. Do you understand?" The man behind the desk swallowed hard. He felt his complexion change as he heard the words of the well-dressed cowboy and shivered from the cold glare of his eyes.

Roger left the motel and drove the Caddy half a mile down the road. He pulled over to the side and adjusted his disguise to appear in his late 60's. He drove back up the road past the motel to get his bearings and then turned the Caddy around once more. Roger had thoughts of breaking into the room and using the element of surprise, but he was not confident the information from the desk clerk was 100% accurate. There was the possibility that there were more than just three kidnappers in the room. He felt the odds of killing three were good, but there was no way to account for a stray bullet. He stopped the car across the two lane highway where the clerk could not see him, just in case he did notice what kind of car Roger was driving. The traffic was becoming heavier and Roger noticed the luncheonette was open and filling up quickly. He decided to pull the Caddy into the luncheonette parking lot and get something to eat while staking out the room. As he began to pull off the gravel he was almost hit by a limousine, which laid on its horn until Roger steered the Caddy back on the shoulder. Startled, Roger checked to see if the road was clear before putting on his left turn signal to enter the parking lot. He saw the limo pull into the motel as he took a space directly in front of the luncheonette. He adjusted his rear view mirror to watch a young, white male dressed in a chauffeur's uniform emerge from the limo. He opened the rear door for a dark complected man who immediately put a top hat on before Roger could get a good look at him. The coifed man reached back inside the car and took a bag from another man in an eggshell suit as he stepped out. His hair was pure white, but he had distinctively Latin features. Roger subtracted twenty years from the man's appearance and was convinced it was Wilfred Benito Sanchez, Bambino de Jackal.

Realizing he had all six of the kidnappers within his grasp, Roger felt a rush of adrenaline. He knew he had to take out the pilot, Eric, to alter their primary escape plan. Roger entered the four-tabled luncheonette and sat on the last stool at the small counter facing room 116. The clerk, who had given him the information an hour earlier, was at the cash register with his coffee and donuts. He did not even take a second look as the old man passed him and sat at the counter near the restrooms. Roger ordered the $2.95 breakfast special, a western omelette, toast, juice, and a bottomless cup of coffee. He made light conversation with the over-worked waitress, and guessed there was only one short order cook in the kitchen. He sat in the busy luncheonette for almost forty minutes before seeing any activity from room 116. Finally, at 9:10 a.m. the door opened and a Spanish woman in her early thirties stepped out with two American men. One was the chauffeur of the limo, a red-haired man in his early 20's about six feet tall with a slender build. The other was a few inches shorter, but exceptionally handsome with a perfect physique. The threesome entered the restaurant and seated themselves without waiting for the table to be cleared. They were less than ten feet from the old man in the corner. Roger put a $5.00 bill on the counter and told the waitress no change was necessary. She thanked him and refilled his coffee as the red-headed chauffeur walked to the men's room. The luncheonette was starting to empty out and Roger signaled for one more cup. He knew he could only sip on the coffee a few minutes longer. The threesome was becoming more boisterous, something about the Spanish girl's sexual preference, when Roger drained his coffee. He stood to leave and geriatrically stretched his arms and legs. His movement caught the attention of the threesome, who made a joke at the old man's expense. The good looking man, who was referred to as Eric by his friends, walked behind him to the men's room. Knowing this was the opportunity he was waiting for, and that there was no one else in the restroom, Roger limped toward the lavatory.

The bathroom was small, with a single stall on the right, a sink on the left and a urinal across from the door. When the old man entered the one called Eric was relieving himself at the urinal. "I'll be done in a second, old timer," he claimed, glancing over his shoulder to see who entered. Roger thought about blocking the entrance to the men's room from the inside since there were no locks, but changed his mind; knowing it would be over in a few seconds. The old man removed the nine-inch blade from its casing in the back of his trousers, and in one swift, powerful motion thrust the knife through the man's back into his heart while silencing a solitary scream with his left hand.

The man they called Eric collapsed and Roger removed his wallet and set him on the toilet in the stall. He quickly checked himself for traces of blood and limped out of the men's room and out of the luncheonette, giving a wave to the waitress on his way.

Roger knew he only had a few minutes before the dead pilot would be missed, and then found. He entered the Caddy and drove to a service road that ran parallel with the back of the motel. He needed to change his disguise, but was having trouble concentrating. It had been many years since his last killing and the sight of the man's blood on his right hand almost sent him into a panic attack. Not wanting to lose control, Roger closed his eyes, took a deep breath, and counted to 100. When he opened his eyes he surveyed his surroundings, the motel was on his right, no one behind him, and only dry, dusty fields to his left. Recomposed, he removed a few wet naps from the glove compartment, cleaned the knife and its casing, and wiped the dried blood from his right hand. He put the wet naps in a puke and choke bag, containing a few soggy fries and squeezed two ketchup packets over the trash. Roger completed his transformation back to FBI Agent, Coyle and drove the Caddy around the other side of the motel. He disposed of the puke and choke bag and the pilot's wallet in a trash can and backed the car into the hotel parking lot four spots to the right of the limo. The clock on the dash read 10:21 a.m. when he saw the red-headed chauffeur and the Spanish lady emerge from the luncheonette. The looks on their faces and the pace of the walk, indicated something was very wrong in their world.

12

The Spanish woman, Illiana, and the chauffeur, George, entered room 116 and shut the door behind them. They both began to yell that Eric had been killed in the luncheonette. To their surprise, Don Juan commanded them to be quiet. George and Illiana focused their attention on the television program Don Juan was watching so intently. A man sitting behind a news desk was pleading for kidnappers not to kill his little girl. When he concluded his statement an anchorman explained there was a mistake over the identity of the child kidnaped at the Austin library. He went on to explain that the kidnappers original target, the granddaughter of former United States Vice President, Day, was not kidnaped, and the abducted child was the daughter of a wealthy cattle rancher. The anchorman reiterated the rancher's offer of the $100 million reward and confirmed the money was on deposit in the First Bank of Austin. Don Juan shut the television off and turned his attention to Illiana and George.

"Did you say Eric has been killed?" he asked. They retraced the events at the diner with Don Juan and said neither of them noticed anyone who might have been a threat.

"When I went into the bathroom and found Eric in the stall I checked to see if his wallet was with him, it wasn't," George added.

"So this could be a simple case of robbery," Kabiv interjected.

"Let's kill the little bitch and cut bait. I don't like this, our ride out of the country is history!" Jesus exclaimed. Don Juan paced the floor and posed a few more questions.

"You said there was an old man with a limp in the cafe?"

"Yes," Illiana and George answered.

"Did you see what type of car he was driving?" Both answered no. George had been rubbing the inside of Illiana's thigh while Eric was in the men's room, listening to promises of what she was going to do for him later. "Maybe coincidence, maybe not, but I think you'll all agree that this job was risky when we decided to take it," Don Juan said. "Sorry Kabiv, but our agenda has changed. Our people have already told us that the American government has not made any efforts to release your friends. Now, with the wrong hostage, we have no political leverage."

"So, what do you say?" the Iranian asked.

"I say we use plan 'B.' Get to the Mexican border via New Mexico, use our people to get us to a country with no extradition agreement with the United States, and collect $100 million as opposed to the $10 million your associates were willing to pay," Don Juan answered.

"No! No!" Kabiv protested, "we have deal! We get the three wrongly accused people out of filthy American jail!" Don Juan knew Kabiv was the only member of the team that was not motivated by money. Sensing he was going to be a problem, Don Juan pulled a pistol from his eggshell suit and shot Kabiv between the eyes. He re-holstered the weapon and walked over to the little girl, who was awakened by the gun shot.

"What's your name?" Don Juan asked. With a slur in her voice from the sedatives she mumbled,

"Tris Brown."

"Yes my dear, you are our $100 million baby."

Don Juan ordered Illiana to cut back on the drugs, he did not want anything to happen to his golden goose. "Jesus, change clothes with George, you will be my chauffeur. George and Illiana, take the $100 million baby with you in the Pathfinder. Go to the alternate rendezvous site outside of Deming, New Mexico and check in as Mr. and Mrs. Clark." George, Illiana and Jesus looked down at Kabiv's body. No one argued. "It's a 400 mile drive to Deming, if you leave now you should get there around 8:00 p.m. Jesus and I will try to make a connection to cross the border and get out of Mexico, we'll meet you in Deming between 9:00 a.m. and 11:00 a.m. tomorrow."

The sound of the gunshot brought Roger's worst fears to the forefront of his mind. His emotions urged him to rush the room and kill everything in sight, but his instincts assured him there would be time for that later, and to play the hand out. On Friday at 11:03 a.m., Roger watched as Jesus, now dressed as a chauffeur, opened the door of the limo for Don Juan. The other American, dressed in clothes that were too small for him, followed a few steps behind. Illiana and Tris exited a moment later and Tris was guided into the back seat of a dark blue Pathfinder. Roger only caught a glimpse of his daughter, but he still had to fight back his tears. The Iranian never came out of the room. Roger knew what the shot was about.

The limo went one way and the Pathfinder another. Roger followed the Pathfinder at a safe distance until it became clear they were headed south on a large interstate. He pulled in front of their vehicle and kept it under surveillance, a trick he learned from the CIA. Before calling Taylor to bring him up to speed on the latest developments, Roger pondered why the Iranian was killed. He turned on the radio and hit the scan button, within seconds he heard his voice pleading for his daughter's safe return. 'They bought it.' As Galahad, he saw the end of intelligence work for country and God with the demise of 'the evil empire.' He knew better than any other spook how to capitalize on his past service; but even at the end, after his naivete was stripped away by the greedy politicians and corporate CEO's, Roger still performed the work out of a sense of patriotism. He knew most black ops outside the U.S. were performed by hired mercenaries, with the exception of a few religious factions from the middle east. It was now obvious the kidnappers went to the highest bidder, and Kabiv was not in it for the money. It made sense that Bambino de Jackal would kill him, more of a cut for him and his crew, and less baggage. He was certain the Jackal wanna-be and his lackey, Jesus, were headed to the same destination as the pathfinder via a different route. They would draw less attention to themselves traveling separately, at a quick glance one would think the Pathfinder was carrying an American man with his Spanish wife and child. The scheme also allowed Don Juan more time to make arrangements to collect the $100 million and get out of the country.

Friday morning was the worst morning the Assistant Chief of Staff ever had in his life. After barely sleeping the night before, he was being bombarded with phone calls from every agency he had reached out to on the Day case. No one knew what was going on, and that made everyone very skiddish. He screamed at Taylor at the FBI three times over the last two hours. He didn't know why, it wasn't Taylor's fault that Galahad did not call, or that he started running a TV ad pleading for the safe return of his daughter (which was picked up by every news station in civilization and being run non-stop). The White House released a statement to cover its own ass, referring everything back to the FBI, which in turn had the Director of the FBI down Grady's throat. To top everything off, he and Sullivan were scheduled to see #1 in five minutes.

The men entered the Oval Office to see the President hanging up the phone. He stood up, shouting,

"What the fuck is going on, Grady!!" Grady bit his lip and almost messed himself.

"We don't know, sir"

"What does that mean?" #1 scolded.

"We haven't heard from Galahad since last night. We don't have any confirmation why that newscast was released, or who released it. The only thing we know for sure is it started out of Austin," Grady replied. The President was silent for a moment, then in a much more controlled voice asked,

"Ellis, what do you *think* it means?" Grady took a deep breath and chose his words carefully.

"Pure conjecture, sir, but if I were Galahad, I would want to buy more time and make the kidnappers think they have other options."

"I don't understand," #1 said.

"I would guess it was Galahad's insurance against the cover of Vice President, Day's granddaughter being kidnaped not holding up, or. . ."

"Or what?" the President asked.

"His insurance against leaks inside the government," Grady finished.

"Do we know if his daughter is still alive?" Chief of Staff, Sullivan asked.

"We don't know anything. Even his location is speculative."

"Why is that?" #1 asked.

"He gave his location to Taylor too freely."

"What are you going to do?" the President asked.

"I've made arrangements with the FBI to monitor all the calls to the First Bank of Austin to see if we can develop any leads. But that might be like trying to find a needle in a haystack, they received over 4000 phone calls from individuals claiming to be the kidnappers in the last half hour," Grady said.

"Galahad knew his little television debut would cause the crazies to come out of the woodwork," Sullivan commented.

"Exactly, making it harder for the kidnappers to make contact. Remember, Galahad said he would be willing to deal with a country with no extradition agreement with the United States. Along with 'all the crazies', as you put it, it's going to take the kidnappers more time to get their plan in motion. That's what I think Galahad wants, if he's still alive," Grady finished. The President dismissed the men with orders to get back to him immediately with any new developments.

Roger picked up his cell phone and dialed the ranch to reach FBI Agent, Taylor. Taylor looked at the ringing phone and prayed to God it was not the Assistant Chief of Staff.

"FBI, Taylor," he answered, cringing.

"I gather you're getting some serious heat from D.C.," Brown said. Taylor let out a sigh of relief.

"That's the understatement of the century."

"I guess my television debut is making the boys in D.C. a little nervous."

"To put it mildly, yes. Where the fuck are you?" Taylor asked.

"Calm down. It appears the kidnappers bought the reward," Brown stated.

"How do you know that?" Taylor asked.

"Let's just say I have them in my sights," Brown answered.

"I guess were going to do it your way"

"My daughter."

"But there are six of them and only one of you," Taylor retorted.

"Well, there are only four of them now," Brown said.

"You took two out?" Taylor questioned.

"No, only one, the pilot. Sanchez took out the Iranian."

"I don't understand," Taylor said.

"I took out the pilot so they couldn't fly out of the country. Sanchez took out the Iranian because the Iranians were out bid."

"I see," Taylor said. "I have to report back to D.C."

"Go ahead, but be alert; I hope to call in the Calvary in the next 24 hours."

"We'll be ready," Taylor assured him.

"Good." The phone went dead in Taylor's hand.

13

Taylor called Grady and relayed the information Brown gave him.

"What do you mean there are only four kidnappers left?" Grady asked, "Did he kill two of them?"

"That's unclear, sir. Brown indicated his television appearance caused some infighting among the kidnappers," Taylor answered.

"He put you on notice, so I guess this operation will be coming to an end shortly. You up for the challenge?" Grady asked.

"Yes, sir, we'll try to put this to bed quickly," Taylor replied.

"Good," Grady said, and hung up the phone.

Grady dialed the President's secretary and asked for an appointment, to his surprise, he received one within the hour. Like a good little assistant, Grady called Sullivan and briefed him on his conversation with Taylor. Sullivan told Grady he would meet him in #1's office in thirty minutes. President Burke listened as Grady reported the new developments.

"Damn, Charles Beuhler was right, this guy is the best. Keep helping Galahad, hopefully things will work out for everyone," #1 ordered.

"Mr. President, outside of acting as a therapist for Galahad to talk to, we haven't done anything to help him directly; but I'll make sure, if and when he calls, we respond quickly," Grady ended. The President looked at his watch, it was approaching 2:15 p.m.

"Good. I'm taking the first lady to Camp David in a couple hours. Use your discretion, if something of a crisis develops call me, if not, I'm sure Tom can handle everything until Sunday evening. I'll expect a full briefing when I return."

"Sir?" Sullivan asked.

"Yes, Tom," #1 responded, with the implication of 'make it quick'.

"I think it would be wise to start considering how to put Galahad back in the deep freeze if he is successful rescuing his daughter."

"Yes, I thought about that. Have the intelligence agencies come up with some scenarios. After it's all said and done we'll invite Mr. Beuhler back and pick his brain on how to deal with Galahad."

The sun was beginning to set on the nation's capital as the limo pulled in front of the Kennedy Memorial. The Chief of Staff exited the car in the twilight and walked toward the eternal flame. He stopped short of the memorial entrance and sat on a park bench next to an elderly man.

"I gather things are going well." the old man stated.

"Perfect. I need you to apply more pressure on Kelley. Let him blackmail me again, this time I won't cooperate and he'll be forced to turn over what he thinks is very damaging evidence," the Chief of Staff stated.

"Very wise. This third rate operator will think he played his trump card with you, and when it has no effect on your standing in the political arena he will kick himself in the ass. I'm sure he'll eventually come to the conclusion that you cut your own deal with his 'very important client' and cut him out of the loop," the old man commented. "But I think it may be in your best interest to still throw Kelley a bone now and then, one never knows when he might be useful."

"#1 is open to ideas on how to resolve the problem of our special friend, he may call upon you for some insight," Sullivan said.

"Marvelous. Our friends around the world will surely appreciate our efforts. They will most likely want you to succeed me as CEO," the old man said.

"I'm not sure if that's what I want. It may be best for our friends if I stay on the inside, and let someone like Day take over as CEO," Sullivan replied.

"I understand your thoughts, but you'll only be on the inside for a little more than two years. The position of CEO is like the position of pope, you'll remain in power until death."

"I appreciate your confidence, but I feel I can be more effective if I have a free hand to change direction when necessary," Sullivan countered.

"You will be 68 years old in a month. Are you sure this is what you want?"

"I'm sure."

"Let it be said, let it be done. I will arrange for Kelley to blackmail you again and inform our friends that their interests would be better served if Day replaces me at my demise," the old man said.

"Day is a good choice, we both know that," the Chief of Staff said.

"He is, but I feel you let your sexual preference dictate your advancement. When #1 wants to meet with me we will guide his good soul as to what to do with Galahad."

"I understand," Sullivan said, as he rose from the bench. He strolled for a few minutes and returned to the limousine.

Roger kept the Pathfinder under surveillance with trained precision. Each time the kidnappers exited or turned, Roger would travel a quarter mile in the opposite direction before doubling back and resuming his pursuit. As darkness overtook the New Mexico desert, Roger was able to relax a little. The cat and mouse games ended in a border town called Deming, where the Pathfinder pulled into a Holiday Inn. Roger caught another glimpse of Tris as she walked into the hotel. He waited a few minutes and then removed his valet from the trunk and checked in under the name of Thomas James. Once in his room, Roger changed into the suit he packed and adjusted his disguise. He was reminiscent of a Wayne Newton impersonator, with jet black hair and a thin mustache. He walked through the hotel and bribed a bellboy to secure the room number of the American with the Spanish wife and little girl. He strolled down the corridor and stopped outside room 218, registered to Mr. and Mrs. Clark. He heard muffled voices, but could not make out the conversation. Suddenly the female voice rose and he recognized it from the diner, it was Illiana. 'I'm tired of babysitting, I'm going down to the lounge to unwind. You watch our golden goose real good and I'll take care of your tiny pecker when I get back.' Roger hurried away from the door and took the stairs down to the hotel lobby.

The handful of people in the lounge were being entertained by a Mexican trio, who were a step below a wedding band, trying to play Bob Seger's 'Old Time Rock and Roll.' Roger sat at the far end of the bar, giving him a panoramic view of the lounge and lobby. Illiana entered moments later dressed in a tight pair of black jeans and a loose fitting blouse, leaving Roger to wonder whether she was wearing a bra or not. She sat in a booth close to the entrance and ordered a cocktail.

"What'll you have?" the bar keep asked.

"Scotch, on the rocks," Roger replied, tossing a ten dollar bill on the bar. He sat and observed his surroundings, watching several of the locals trying to make time with Illiana to no avail. Roger signaled the bartender.

"Send the lady in the white blouse another drink and have a scotch delivered to her table," Roger ordered. He put a twenty on the bar as he left, "keep the change." Roger walked directly over to the booth.

"May I?" he asked.

"It's a free country and I don't own the booth," she replied in perfect English, which somewhat surprised him. Roger thought of Agent Taylor's warning as he slid in the booth, 'she fucks her marks to death, literally.' The bar maid delivered the two drinks right on queue and Roger tipped her five dollars.

"Pretty sure of ourselves, aren't we?" the kidnapper remarked.

"I know what I like," Roger replied.

"Oh, you couldn't handle it!" the kidnapper laughed. Roger removed ten $100 bills from his suit coat pocket and said,

"I'll pay a thousand dollars to find out." The kidnapper looked at the money and thought about his proposition.

"Right to the point, I like that. You're not a cop, because even the best vice cops don't wear $3000 suits. You have a room?" she asked, as she reached for the money. Roger pulled the money back and counted out five hundred dollars.

"Yes, I have a room, but you only get half now. The other half once we're inside, understood?" Illiana took the $500.

"Fair enough." They each took a sip of their drink and headed out of the club. On the way to the elevator the kidnapper asked,

"What's your name?"

"My name is of no importance to you, nor is yours to me. I just want a good fuck, nothing kinky, just a good fuck, and you looked like the best prospect for my desires."

"Fair enough. You're going to get the fuck of your life," the kidnapper responded. The elevator doors opened on the fourth floor and the twosome walked down the hall to Roger's room. He looked at his watch as he unlocked the door, it was 11:45 p.m. Roger shut and locked the door and turned to see the kidnapper had opened her blouse, exposing her firm breasts. He used his momentum turning away from the door to hit her with a roundhouse and send her crashing, unconscious, to the floor.

When Roger revived Illiana with smelling salts she found herself naked and gagged, tied to a chair. Her vision was blurred, but she recognized that the man standing above her was not the same man who propositioned her in the lounge. This man had lighter hair, no mustache, and was dressed for a round of golf. Roger had his shoulder holster over his shirt with his weapon in full view. In his left hand he held a knife and in his right a pair of wire cutters.

"Do you know who I am?" Roger questioned. Only semi conscious, the kidnapper shook her head. "I am the father of the little girl you and your friends are holding hostage," Roger stated. The kidnapper strained to focus through her swollen, tearing eyes. She began to remember the man who put up the ransom money, not from his appearance, but from his voice, which she heard many times on the drive from Dalhart to Deming. "Let me inform you of something, you are going to die." Roger's words had no noticeable effect on the kidnapper.

"It's up to you how much pain you want to endure before your death." He knelt down in front of Illiana to ensure she had a good view of the knife and wire cutters. "I know about Eric, Jesus, George, Kabiv and Wilfred Benito Sanchez, or Don Juan as you call him." Sanchez' name drew a reaction from the kidnapper. She looked up with naked eyes that asked, 'who are you?' "You will tell me everything I want to know or die the most painful death imaginable." With a flash of dramatics, Roger said, "Oh, I'm sorry. You're probably wondering how I know all of you so intimately, permit me introduce myself." He moved to within two inches of her face and in a cold voice said, "In some circles, a few years back, my associates called me Galahad."

The information took a second to register, but once it clicked she became fear stricken and tried to scream and break loose from her bonds. Roger responded with a back-handed slap, gashing her face open with the wire clippers. He tortured her for an hour before she gave him what he thought to be all the pertinent information she knew. Before begging Roger to kill her, he cut off three fingers, four toes, stabbed her six times, and fucked her with the blade of his knife. He killed her humanely by snapping her neck. While cleaning up the room and disposing of the body in the bathtub, Roger decided it was time to rush room 218 and get Tris. He would take care of Don Juan and Jesus later. Roger cleaned the blood off the carpet, so at first glance no one would suspect any wrong doing, and put on his good ol' cowboy disguise. He put the 'Do Not Disturb' sign on the door and carried his valet to the Caddy.

It was 2:08 a.m. when Roger approached room 218. He knew Don Juan and Jesus called just minutes before the now deceased Illiana went to the lounge. He also knew they arranged for a connection to cross the Mexican border and would arrive at the hotel between 9:00 a.m. and 11:00 a.m. on Saturday morning. Roger placed the silencer on his gun and used Illiana's key to enter the room. He opened the door slowly and let his eyes adjust to the darkness. The curtains were half open and the eerie green glow from the neon Holiday Inn sign illuminated the front of the room. Roger kept an eye on the two double beds as he shut and locked the door. The bed closest to the entrance had a large figure lying in it and the bed next to the window had the scant outline of a child. Wanting no mistake, Roger leaped on the first bed and grabbed for the figures groin. His left hand prized a fistful of testicles. Before the man could scream, Roger's right hand, holding the gun, came crashing down on the kidnappers face. Roger quickly snapped the man's neck, wrapped his body in a blanket, and stuck it in the closet.

Not knowing if the half open curtains were a signal to let the other two kidnappers know everything was okay, Roger decided to leave them open. He knelt beside Tris's bed, pulled back the covers, and checked her vitals. She was still sound asleep and he knew she had to be drugged. Every morning, when he played bronco daddy at the ranch, he tried to sneak into her room, but to no avail; she would always awaken before Roger got to the bed.

Roger woke his Tris at 8:00 a.m. on Saturday morning. Between the haze of the drugs and the disguise of the good ol' cowboy, it took him the better part of a half hour to convince her it was daddy. There were no big hugs, just an understanding of who he was. Roger realized he could use her dulled senses to his advantage. He told Tris they were going to play a game where she would hide in the tub between pillows and blankets. Roger told her she could go back to sleep if she wanted to, but under no circumstances was she allowed to lift her head above the top of the tub. Tris was happy to fall back asleep in her new bed. Roger knew the plastic tub would not stop a bullet, but under the circumstances it was the best he could come up with.

It was approaching 9:00 a.m. Roger unlocked the door and pondered the possibility that the other two kidnappers might double cross their own. He replaced George's dead body in the bed and arranged a few pillows and towels under the covers of the other bed. The more he thought about the double cross, the more confident he became that Bambino de Jackal would want the entire $100 million for himself and his sidekick. Roger hid in the closet, next to the entrance of the bathroom, and left the door ajar. He wanted both men to step in and shut the door behind them before he opened fire. At 9:25 a.m. the door opened and the man in the chauffeur uniform entered. A man in a dark business suit with dark brown hair followed closely behind him. As soon as the dark-haired man shut the door, Jesus fired three rounds into George's corpse. The dark haired man, with his gun drawn, ordered Jesus to get the child. As Jesus hopped over the first bed he heard the sound of two gunshots. He looked toward the door and saw the dark-haired man falling backward with two small bullet holes in his forehead. Before he could react, Jesus heard three of Roger's four shots and felt a fiery pain in his chest. Roger returned George's body to the closet, where he was joined by Bambino de Jackal and Jesus. When he moved the corpses, he reflected that Sanchez' disguise was wanting. Roger woke Tris and played with her until she was coherent enough to walk. At 10:15 a.m., on a beautiful September morning, the ol' cowboy strolled out of the Deming Holiday Inn with his granddaughter. The twosome got in the late model Caddy and headed east, toward Texas.

14

Roger Brown's main concern on the 600 mile trip home was his daughter's health. He stopped at a puke and choke for lunch an hour outside of Deming. The Coke and cheeseburger seemed to help her shake off some of the sedatives. He told Tris he was practicing for a Halloween party and changed back into an FBI agent. This time his cover was Agent Robert Galahad, not David Coyle. She asked a few questions, mostly concerning her mother, and then drifted back to sleep.

It was time for damage control. He picked up the cellular and called William Buck, again hoping Bill picked up the phone himself.

"Hello?" Buck said.

"Bill, Roger here."

"Did you find Tris?" Buck asked.

"I can't go into that now," Roger replied. "How much of the deposit for the television broadcast has been used?"

"A little over half," Buck said.

"Good, keep running it until you use up the $20 million," Roger ordered.

"Okay," Buck answered.

"I hate to impose on you, but I need another favor."

"Anything, what do you need?" Buck asked.

"Arrange for Cathy to be transferred from LBJ to my ranch with whatever medical care she needs. Pay any expenses out of the remaining deposit. Ask the police to escort the ambulance to the property line of the ranch, but no further - that's important," Roger emphasized.

"Okay, I can handle that," Buck said.

"I'll arrange for her protection from the property line in," Roger said. "Make sure you get her there at exactly 10:00 p.m. tonight, no earlier, no later.

"Got it, no problem. I'll use what pull I have to take care of this. Anything else?" Buck asked.

"No, and thank you," Roger said. He clicked off the phone before Buck could make another inquiry.

Roger reached behind him and grabbed the knapsack off the back seat. He retrieved a little purple address book from the velcroed side pouch and proceeded to make a series of ten phone calls as Joe Wilson. Two of the ten men he tried to contact were dead, and one had been rendered a paraplegic from a work related accident. The calls were to the former Green Berets who served under him in the hell that is now called the Vietnam conflict. Over the past twenty years, Roger helped each one of the soldiers in one way or another, most times without their knowledge. In one case it was having a charge against a former sergeant, who inadvertently killed a man in a bar room brawl, reduced to manslaughter and helping his family financially during his three and a half-year incarceration. Wilson helped another overcome drug addiction, and yet another settle the demons of his past. Deep in the hearts of the remaining men, they knew Wilson looked after them since their military service ended. Needless to say, none of them bought the cover story of his death. Roger opened each conversation with the same words, 'Everyone in, everyone out,' no man had to question who was on the line. He asked each of them for a favor and assured them they would be well compensated. Four of the former Berets said they could be at the ranch by 7:00 p.m. that evening, the other three could arrive by 1:00 a.m. Sunday morning. Wilson told the group of four the ambulance would be arriving at 10:00 p.m. and indicated their mission was purely a protection operation. He told them where to find weapons, if needed, and to use the code name Galahad to the housekeeper. Roger had kept track of his former soldiers after the fall of Vietnam and was sure none of them were connected to any counter-intelligence agencies. The fact that the highest ranking of the seven was discharged as a master sergeant made Roger feel even more comfortable. He called the ranch and advised the housekeeper that Mrs. Brown would be coming home at 10:00 p.m., and that some men would be arriving to protect them and the ranch. He gave her strict orders not to let anyone into the main house unless they used the password 'Galahad.' Finally, he instructed her to tell the hired hand to take a vacation, immediately.

The hired hand was a Gabby Hayes look-alike who had been with Roger since his transformation from Galahad. The old cowboy, who went by the name Bob, had no family that Roger was aware of and his instincts told him he was not involved. Regardless, he did not feel it was prudent to have the hired hand around in case the situation became sticky. Roger surmised Bob would hop in his old pick-up truck and head for his favorite bordello near the Mexican border, that's what he did the first few times he had a couple days off - Roger knew because he followed the old man.

It was 3:45 p.m. on Saturday afternoon. Tris was still asleep and Roger was making good time on the interstate. He dialed the number of his attorney, Irving Stein.

"Irving, I need a lot of things done very quickly and very discretely," Roger opened, foregoing the normal pleasantries.

"I'm sorry for your misfortune," Stein replied.

"Thank you," Brown said. This was the most personal conversation the two men ever shared. "First, after you hang up with me, have this cell number lost. I know it's under a fictitious name, but I want you to run it at least five degrees of separation from any of my trusts or aliases. The same goes for the California plates," Roger said.

"Fine. That will be very expensive," Stein noted.

"Then I want you to do the same with alias David Coyle and alias Thomas James. You know the routine, run payments for everything through one of the off shore accounts, back to Europe, then Asia, then Switzerland. . . . It's very important there is no traceability to me, or you."

"I understand. This will also be very expensive," Stein stated, in an even voice.

"Fine. Use the seven digit account from the Swiss bank to cover all expenses, then bring back the Swiss alias of Sir Robert Galahad," Roger ordered.

"Do you think that's wise, sir?" Stein asked.

"Bring Sir Robert Galahad back with a splash, lots of noise. I want whomever is listening to know Galahad is back," Roger said.

"Fine. Anything else?"

"Yes, has anyone approached you about Galahad in the last few years?" Roger asked.

"Only after Galahad reported to me that the Swiss were holding billions of dollars that rightfully belonged to holocaust victims, but they were only fishing for information," Stein answered. "I'm very indebted to you for that service. Is there anything else I can do for you?" Roger, speaking more to himself than Stein, asked, "I wonder why they have not tried to turn you." Stein answered matter of factly,

"For several reasons. First, I am an Israeli citizen and don't travel in the same circles or have the same aspirations. Second, they know you have compensated me in ways they cannot. Lastly, I'm sure they know I fear and respect you more than them."

"When can I expect all this to be done?" Roger asked.

"By 6:00 p.m. on Sunday." Before Roger could hang up the phone, Stein uttered, "good luck."

Roger met Stein right after Joe Wilson turned into a spook named Galahad. Stein was involved with the Mesad, but was more of a young legal counsel than a spook. Galahad worked very well with the Mesad, U.S. spooks had to. As Galahad's legend grew, so did the Jewish attorneys who relocated to Philadelphia. The inner circles of the intelligence world learned to respect one another when Galahad began to capitalize on his efforts. Stein, who was insulated politically and brilliant financially, helped Galahad establish a trust and multiple aliases as an insurance policy in the event he ever wanted out. In the early 90's, before Galahad retired, he had a fling with a German woman who mentioned she heard a Swiss banker speak of billions of dollars that suddenly appeared in April of 1945. After some investigation, which was concurrent with his mission for the National Security Agency, Galahad stumbled across hard evidence of the Nazi's depositing large sums of money in Swiss banks. The records indicated a large percentage of the deposits were confiscated from detained Jews in the 1930's and 40's. When Galahad returned to the United States, he passed the information on to Stein, who informed his contacts in the Mesad. The information Galahad unearthed formed the backbone of the restitution of the Swiss banks to the holocaust victims in the mid '90's. Stein, who never divulged the source of the information, was elevated to the top of his profession as a lawyer and power broker in the eyes of Israeli intelligence agencies. Roger was above reproach in Stein's eyes, out of respect, gratitude and fear.

Shortly after Roger hung up the phone with Stein, Tris awoke and informed her father she was hungry and had to go to the bathroom. A stop at another puke and choke resolved both problems. Tris was still feeling the effects of the drugs and fell right to sleep as soon as she climbed back in the car. Roger took the opportunity to begin the process of destroying any evidence that connected him to the pursuit and rescue of his daughter. He removed the California plates from the Caddy and replaced them with his own Texas plates. Using the wire cutters, Roger tediously cut the California plates into tiny pieces and disposed of them along the interstate. He removed the blade of the knife from its handle, thoroughly cleaned both, and jettisoned them from the Caddy miles apart. Roger did the same with the gun after destroying the barrel and silencer beyond repair to avoid any possibility of ballistics testing. By the time he was three hours from his ranch, any evidence connecting him to Tris's recovery was spread along a 200 mile stretch of Texas highway, some in the dry dust and some in rivers.

Roger was ecstatic he had his baby back and confident that Buck would take care of having Cat transferred to the ranch. He didn't need to worry about her safety because he knew his former Green Beret comrades would give their lives to protect her. Relieved his daughter and wife were safe, Roger began to go over the events of the last three and a half days. He could not vanquish the thought that Tris was the original target of the kidnappers from the start. The ordeal of rescuing Tris from her captors was extremely difficult, or was it? Could it have been the emotional strain of the mark being his own flesh and blood, and the fact that he was physically and mentally out of shape for the mission that magnified the difficulty of the rescue? He did catch a few breaks along the way. Peggy Short's electronic diary gave complete descriptions of the kidnappers and their plan, it was almost as if it was designed for him to find. If someone was handling Roger, they would have known her journal contained all the information he needed to catch them. That someone would also know Roger, or Galahad, would kill them. If someone was handling him, that someone had to know he was Galahad, and only Buehler could make that connection for certain. Former Vice President, Day knew Galahad, but he did not know Roger Brown, for Day to come after him he would have had to persecute himself. However, Roger did not overlook the possibility that it could have been a combination of the two. He decided Robert Galahad would pay a visit to Charles Buehler after he settled things at the ranch.

When Roger arrived at his Austin home, the clock on the dash read 12:04 a.m. As he drove the Caddy down the access road toward the main house he was stopped by one of the Green Berets carrying an M-16. He used the password 'Galahad' and drove into the car port next to the rear entrance. Roger dropped his keys in his pocket and carried his sleeping daughter up to her mother in the master bedroom. Remembering his wife in the recovery room, Roger was expecting to see a sorry sight. He was pleasantly surprised to see Cat sitting up in their bed, with only a three inch gauze pad on her right cheek. A look of horror came over Cat's face when she saw the bald-headed man enter the bedroom carrying her daughter. She was relieved when she heard Roger's voice say, 'she's only asleep, she's fine.' He placed Tris on the bed next to her mother and the couple was overcome with emotion. Roger gave Cat a laconic synopsis of his past and explained the strange men guarding the house. He took his wife's hands and said, 'it's still not over, on Monday I'm going to D.C. to try to get to the bottom of this mess.' Cat did not fully comprehend her husband's dissertation, but she knew he needed her support. As Roger was removing his disguise she said, 'I've trusted you with my life and counted on you to bring our baby home. You have never failed me and I won't fail you. Do whatever you have to do.' Roger leaned over his wife and she gently stroked his face as they kissed.

Later that night, Roger called the seven Green Berets together in his office. After getting reacquainted, Roger spelled out their orders.

"First, someone take the nurse back to the hospital. If my wife or daughter require medical attention contact Dr. Francis at LBJ Hospital." One of the seven volunteered to take the nurse back to LBJ. "Next, I want the Caddy stripped completely and make it disappear. I want at least one man at the computer center at all times, but only for two hour shifts." Roger pushed a button on his desk and the oak paneled wall slid back to display six video monitors. After showing each member of the unit how to use the equipment, he ordered, "Three men at all times outside the main house, one here at the monitors, and one reviewing the surveillance tapes of the house from last Monday to now. Rotate positions every two hours when you're not eating or sleeping." Colonel Wilson kept them in the dark about the purpose of their mission. "And I don't have to tell you, protect my wife and child at any cost until I return." Roger ended the session with his comrades and went upstairs. The time on the alarm clock read 3:41 a.m. when he climbed into bed with his wife. His last thought before falling asleep was to call FBI Agent, Taylor first thing in the morning.

15

Roger and Cat spent Sunday relaxing with Tris. Roger played his part of Bronco and Tris rode him without missing a beat. It didn't appear the ordeal had any traumatic effect on her. Although he did not say anything to Cat, Roger was glad Tris was heavily sedated and slept through most of the tribulation. He made a mental note to have her examined by Dr. Francis the following week. It was close to 7:00 p.m. Sunday evening when Roger called Taylor.

"FBI, Taylor."

"Taylor, it's me," Roger said.

"Where have you been?" Taylor asked.

"I've lost their trail," Roger said, in an exaggerated tone. Taylor knew it was a line of bullshit and waited for the trace on the call.

"What do you mean you've lost them?" Taylor asked, in a not-so-convinced voice.

"I lost them at the border," Roger explained.

"Which border?" Taylor asked.

"Right by Eagle Pass," Roger answered, "can you guys help me out?" The computer indicated the call was made from Brown's ranch, just like all the others.

"I've only been your contact, you told us to keep away from this operation," Taylor said, knowing Brown wanted confirmation that the government knew he had his daughter back.

"Do you have any leads at all?" Roger asked.

"Only some news out of southwestern New Mexico of a quadruple homicide," Taylor said. "I don't know if that helps, but you had me ordered to stay in my office since Thursday. I don't get to hear too much in here."

"What does that have to do with me?" Roger asked.

"That's all I have," Taylor said.

"Fine, I'll get back to you later," Roger said, and hung up the phone.

Taylor knew Galahad had his daughter back and he, and every other federal agent, knew that the kidnaping team of six were dead. He called Assistant Chief of Staff, Ellis Grady, who, for the first time, was not in his office. Taylor left a message and Grady called back within ten minutes. Taylor reported his conversation with Brown. The Assistant Chief's responses were much more subdued than during their previous conversations, as if he already knew the answers.

"Taylor, you did record all conversations with Brown, right?" Taylor swallowed hard.

"No, sir, on the contrary, I only spoke to him on a secure line, I had it checked every few hours." Taylor held the phone away from his ear, expecting the bureaucrat from D.C. to start yelling. He was flabbergasted when Grady mildly responded,

"I see. Get back to me when Brown calls again."

Grady called Station Chief, Anthony Bucco, who had filled him in on the events in Dalhart, Texas and Deming, New Mexico. Not finding Bucco in his office, Grady tried him at home. One of his children answered the phone and Grady waited for him to get on the line.

"Hello?"

"Bucco, this is Ellis Grady."

"Yes, sir," he replied.

"Brown called in and said he lost their trail," Grady said, not wanting to go into detail on an unsecured line.

"He's buying time," Bucco answered.

"I know that," Grady responded, angrily. "Was there anything peculiar about the situation?"

"Everything in this case has been peculiar. Hell, even the Treasury had agents in New Mexico," Bucco stated.

"Why's that?" Grady asked.

"They thought there might be some counterfeiting involved."

"Did you buy that?" Grady asked.

"My man in the field didn't," Bucco replied.

"Keep an eye out, I'll get back to you," Grady finished. Grady did not pretend to have the mind of a master sleuth, but he sensed something was wrong. He knew the kidnappers were found dead and Galahad more than likely had secured his daughter, he was informed of those facts 12 hours ago. What didn't sit right was the speed at which all the facts fell into place. How quickly the local police were able to inform the Feds, and how quickly the Feds connected Dalhart to Deming, was alarming. The Assistant Chief of Staff looked back over his notes. It was one of Bucco's agents who tied everything together, but it was unclear how Bucco's parallel investigation received all the information so quickly. He and Chief of Staff, Sullivan were to brief the President at 9:00 p.m. when he returned from Camp David. Grady called Sullivan, who was in his office, and tried to explain his concerns. Sullivan listened but did not seem too interested, he just ordered Grady to bring everything up to #1 at the briefing. He hung up the phone with the sneaking suspicion that if there was going to be a fall guy, it was him.

Grady and Sullivan met as they reached the entrance to the Oval Office. Sullivan knocked and the two men entered. The President was seated behind his desk in his night clothes, ready to retire for the evening.

"Gentlemen, fill me in on our little situation in Austin," #1 said, in a much better mood than when he left on Friday. Ellis Grady began his report,

"FBI Agent, Taylor called me one hour ago and reported that Galahad informed him that he lost the kidnappers trail."

"Really?" the President said, obviously surprised by the development.

"This is in contrast to what the FBI believes," Grady said.

"What does our illustrious Bureau believe?" #1 asked, with more than just a hint of sarcasm in his voice. Grady thought now was the best time to bring up the parallel investigation of Station Chief, Bucco.

"The FBI ran a parallel investigation while Galahad was tracking the kidnappers. The primary reason was to give the impression to the media that everything humanly possible was being done to save the former Vice President's granddaughter. The secondary reason was to have them keep their eyes and ears open for any obvious clues. They were given strict instructions not to become involved," Grady said. The President interrupted,

"A good idea. Yours?"

"Yes, sir. With the help of some unexplained Treasury agents, we've learned that all six members of the kidnaping team are dead and there is no trace of Patricia Brown. We are assuming, for the moment, that Galahad has his daughter back at his ranch outside of Austin."

"You know what assuming can do," the President stated.

"Hopefully by tomorrow we can have confirmation on everything. But things. . ." Sullivan interrupted,

"Sir, I think it's best from here on in we limit the amount of people who know what's going on with Galahad. I have some top secret information regarding this situation that I think would be best discussed alone." Sullivan turned to Grady, "No reflection on you Ellis, I think you did a fine job in this matter."

"Wait a minute Tom," #1 said. "The boy already knows as much as anyone, I want him kept in the loop." He turned to Grady, "Finish what you were saying, son."

"Things don't add up," Grady said.

"Be more specific, Ellis," the President ordered.

"Timing. We, the FBI, knew locations and other information too quickly. I have a call into Treasury to find out why one of their agents was at the scene when four of the bodies were discovered, and how he very graciously drew the dotted lines for the FBI from Dalhart to Deming," Grady answered.

"Does this have anything to do with your top secret information Tom?" #1 asked.

"Yes, sir," the Chief of Staff answered.

"Go on," #1 ordered, settling back in his chair.

"When the whole incident began with Galahad I thought it best to handle the matter as one of national security," Sullivan stated.

"Oh really?" #1 commented.

"Under the premise of national security, I had the NSA use the Anti-Terrorist Division of the Treasury, under the guidance of the CIA, track Galahad and keep him under surveillance," Sullivan stated. The President rose from his chair and slowly paced in front of the sofa in the middle of the Oval Office. After contemplating what his Chief of Staff told him, he chose his words carefully.

"After this ordeal is over, you and I will sit down and revisit what is and what is not considered an event of national security. Then we will take a look at the Constitution to see who is in charge of the government, the Chief of Staff, or the President," #1 scolded. "From this moment on I want it understood that I requested the help of the CIA and NSA, and God help you, Tom if this comes back to bite me in the ass!" Sullivan realized trying to explain his actions would only complicate matters and further enrage his boss.

"Yes, sir."

"What did the NSA and CIA come up with?" #1 asked. Sullivan went through a fifteen minute dissertation, explaining how the undercover Treasury agents picked up Galahad's trail close to Dalhart, Texas. He told #1 about Galahad's other aliases, David Coyle and Thomas James, and produced photographs of the three men, none of which looked anything alike. Sullivan also had pictures of Brown's late model Cadillac, which was registered to a dead man from California. Sullivan closed with a discourse on the sophisticated telecommunication system Galahad used to contact Agent Taylor, including the fact that the cell phone was registered to a corporation in Hong Kong. Grady sat with his mouth agape as he listened to the detailed information the Chief of Staff laid on the table.

"What exactly are you telling me, Tom," #1 asked, looking somewhat perplexed.

"Galahad tracked down the kidnappers, killed them, and took his daughter back to his ranch." He showed the President a fuzzy photo of a man carrying a child in the rear entrance of the house. The photo was time-dated 12:17 a.m. that morning.

"So, why is he still running that TV spot?" #1 asked.

"He's buying time," Grady said.

"Exactly," Sullivan reinforced.

"For what?" the President asked.

"To figure out how to go back in the deep freeze," Sullivan answered.

"Are you sure he did all this?" the President asked both men.

"We're dealing with the best intelligence agent of our time. You heard Buehler, he actually felt sorry for the kidnappers," Sullivan replied. "I think we have 48 hours before the money he paid the television station runs out. The FBI has been instructed to keep a lid on this matter and not allow any interviews; perhaps Charles Buehler could be of some assistance."

"Yes, I hope so," #1 said. "Either way we have a P.R. problem. We cannot let it be known that we encouraged vigilantism, but even more importantly, we don't want Galahad's secrets to surface. Call Mr. Buehler and ask him if he can join us for lunch tomorrow at noon," the President ordered.

"Yes, sir," Sullivan replied. The two men left the Oval Office. As they approached Sullivan's office, the Chief of Staff said,

"Ellis, you did a nice job with this mess, make sure none of your FBI contacts leak anything. And be on time for lunch tomorrow."

"Yes, sir," Grady replied.

Grady made his way back to his own office, which was much smaller, but comfortable. He was 100% sure his contact at the FBI, Bucco, would not be making any public statements. Grady sat behind his desk and put his feet on top of the organized mess. 'Holy fuck,' he said aloud, trying to slow his mind down from what he just heard from Chief of Staff, Sullivan. He still didn't think the facts added up, everything was just too fast. 'Something's rotten in Denmark, old Billy Boy.' For the next three hours, well into Monday morning, Grady went through the time line of the events of the kidnaping step by step. He went as far as drawing a flow chart to indicate where Galahad should have been based on Sullivan's NSA investigation. The fact that Sullivan gave no concrete explanation how they picked up Galahad's trail bothered him. Grady pondered the possibility that it was just a coincidence, or, that like most executives, he really didn't know the specifics. Still, it was too fast. 'As if they knew where he was going,' he said to himself. That thought frightened him; if it was true, it meant there was a conspiracy and Galahad's kid was the target all along. 'Does Galahad have that much on the country and the people in power? What could he possible have on Sullivan?' Grady knew Sullivan for over ten years and outside of rumors of being a closet homosexual, which in today's day and age would not be considered a career-threatening liability, he was an upstanding citizen. What fed his skepticism and rekindled the fires in his gut was Sullivan's use of the NSA and Anti-Terrorist Divisions of the Treasury. Why would he risk his position with #1? He knew his Shakespearian remark was on target, but how? With fatigue setting in and an early call to catch up on his other duties before the luncheon, Grady's conspiracy theory was losing its conviction. 'Probably something I'm missing,' he said to himself, as he prepared to leave. 'But I've never seen Sullivan break the chain of command before.' Be aware and be flexible, he thought. The feeling of being the fall guy had diminished, but deep in his heart he trusted his skepticism.

16

The executive dining room had been prepared for four people, but only the President, Charles Buehler and Assistant Chief of Staff, Ellis Grady were present at noon. The conversation centered around the Monday Night Football game between the Washington Redskins and Dallas Cowboys. Buehler, in his usual way, dominated the conversation.

"When Tom called to invite me here for lunch I told him I had one condition, that he be my guest in my private box for this evening's Redskin's game. I'd like to extend that invitation to you two gentlemen also," Buehler said.

"I'd love to Charles, but I'm afraid I have other commitments," the President declined.

"Mr. Grady?" Buehler asked, as if to say 'don't be shy'.

"Mr. Buehler I'd be honored, but I'll have to take a rain check," Ellis said, hinting it was impossible for him to get away. Sullivan entered the executive dining room at 12:20 p.m.

"I apologize Mr. President," Sullivan said, as he walked over and extended his hand to Charles Buehler. "I just received some information about why we're here today and wanted to get my facts straight." This was as good an opportunity as any to discuss the highly sensitive nature of Galahad. "The CIA's Anti-Terrorist Division received information from their liaison at Interpol. They claim that one Sir Robert Galahad of Switzerland has been making a lot of contacts throughout the world, they've confirmed eight flights out of Austin, one of them to Washington D.C."

"What does this mean?" the President asked.

"An olive branch, perhaps," Buehler offered. Sullivan and Grady updated the aging power broker on the Galahad reports, all of which were now confirmed.

"You see Charles, we have a dilemma any way we choose to go with Mr. Galahad," the President stated. "Sooner or later the truth about the kidnaping of his daughter is going to surface, and even though we are ecstatic about the safe return of his child, we cannot condone his methods; vigilantism and anarchy would run rampant. On the other hand, if we do anything to aggravate Mr. Galahad, I'm afraid whatever information he has would become public. I need to know how damaging the information would be to the United States Government, and I would appreciate your professional opinion on the best way to handle this situation. Buehler paused from his minestrone soup and sat back in his chair.

"I see," he said, in a long breath. After a moment he answered slowly, "Mr. President, without going into detail, for then I would be exposing people who have entrusted me for years, the answer to the first part of your question is quite clear cut. Galahad's information would bring diplomatic relations with all of our allies to an end, immediately. It would probably mean the end of our government as we know it."

"Could you be a little more precise?" the President asked. "Exactly what does 'the end of our government as we know it' mean?"

"The why's and how's, no; but the theory is better than 50/50," Buehler stated firmly, making it clear he would help, but not at the expense of being a canary.

"Then how do we handle Galahad?" the Chief of Staff asked.

"That's a problem. I believe Galahad wants to go back in his so called 'deep freeze,' the status quo, but I see in your situation it's not that easy. The leaks emanating from within our government will eventually flow to the media and the truth about the six dead kidnappers will surface. I'm sure this administration does not want to get involved with a cover up, like Nixon," Buehler said.

"Exactly," #1 reinforced, "but I don't want to destroy our government either."

"Have you considered letting the chips fall where they may and killing three birds with one stone?" Buehler asked, tauntingly.

"I don't follow you," the President said.

"The administration announces the safe return of the kidnaped child and then lets the Justice Department do its job of charging Galahad with the murders of the six kidnappers, that's the first bird. It keeps the administration austere and at an arm's length from the kidnaping and Galahad. I believe most Americans will side with Galahad and the administration will take a little hit on the public opinion polls; but any first year law student will be able to have him acquitted on the basis of justifiable homicide due to temporary insanity. That's the second bird. The publicity from the trial, along with a modicum of input from the people who would be exposed if the information surfaced, will paint Galahad as a lunatic. That's the third bird, gentlemen, his allegations will never be taken seriously by our allies."

"It still sounds like a conspiracy to me," Chief of Staff Sullivan stated.

"Not at all, Tom," Buehler replied, "the President and his administration do everything by the book. The people who could be exposed do not fall under the same rules and regulations as a government body, they are free to spend their money anyway they care to; I believe that's in the Constitution," Buehler ended.

"But what about Galahad's past as a Green Beret and a spook?" Grady asked.

"What past? Galahad himself made sure there were no connections to his past by destroying all evidence," Buehler answered.

"And Roger Brown does not exist more than seven years ago," Grady finished.

"Remember son, we used the witness protection program. I believe for those files to be opened it would have to escalate to the Supreme Court, which could be a nice touch on our problem. We could capitalize on that opportunity to imply that Roger Brown was an informant, or even better yet, a former KGB

Agent," Buehler stated, pleased with himself. The President, who was not completely assured by Buehler's solution, shook his head and asked,

"Is there any other possible resolution?"

"No, sir, not without doing a major cover up that would put you at personal risk," Buehler replied.

"I really don't have the stomach to hang a three-time Congressional Medal of Honor winner out to dry, but any interference on my behalf would be considered obstruction of justice," the President moaned.

"The crux of the problem is not Galahad, but leaks to the media; I agree that if you do not prosecute Galahad for taking the law into his own hands you're setting a precedent for anarchy. Besides, there's a chance that Galahad might go along with this so he can return to his life as Roger Brown. Let's not forget, he was not a choir boy when he was a spook."

Roger spent his entire morning on the phone. He called Bill Buck, told him to cease running the TV spot at midnight on Monday night, and thanked him again for all his help. He contacted the First Bank of Austin and instructed them to deposit the $100 million transferred from his trust, and the $2.8 million representing the unused portion of the deposit to the television station, into short term CD's. Using the secured line, Roger chartered a plane from Texas to B.W.I. for 7:00 p.m. that evening. On his third attempt, Roger finally reached Dr. Francis at LBJ Hospital and persuaded her to stop by and look at his wife. He dispensed one of the Green Berets for her transportation. His final call was to Stein, advising him that he may drop in on Tuesday or Wednesday.

Dr. Francis arrived around noon on Monday to examine Cathy. She changed her bandages and told her she was progressing remarkably well.

"I wish she were still in the hospital," the doctor stated.

"Circumstances, doc," Roger replied. "Will she need any ongoing medical attention?"

"Not unless she starts to run a fever or something out of the ordinary comes up," Dr. Francis replied. "I'll check on her at the end of the week."

"Good. I need your discretion, and not the hypothetical type either," Roger stated.

"On what?" the attractive female surgeon asked, with a trace of an English accent.

"I would like you to look at someone else while you are here and not ask any questions, things are not as they appear." The doctor hesitated.

"You mean off the record?"

"Yes," Roger replied.

"Alright," the doctor said, "but my bill is going to be double."

"Fine," Roger said, as he led the doctor to Tris's room. She gave Tris a complete physical, including a neurological exam, and drew two vials of blood. Roger explained the ordeal she had been through, leaving out the explanation of her return.

"She's a beautiful girl, everything seems normal. I'll have the blood analyzed and will only contact you if there is a problem," the doctor said.

"Thank you," Roger answered. He paid her in cash and had the Beret drive her back to LBJ.

Later that afternoon, Roger met with his Green Berets and discussed basic strategies in the event of an emergency. He also informed the men each would be paid $1000 per day for his service. When the meeting adjourned, Roger gathered his spook items and packed for three nights. He said his goodbyes to his wife and daughter and drove one of the ranch's pick-up trucks to the airport to meet the 7:00 p.m. charter.

The game between the Cowboys and the Redskins was intense, with Dallas ahead 10-7 at the half.

Well, how are things?" the old man asked.

"Very well," the Chief of Staff replied. "#1 will have a joint press conference with the director of the FBI at 11:00 a.m. on Tuesday."

"Good," Buehler replied.

"On Wednesday the Justice Department will announce its investigation, and a warrant for Brown's arrest will be issued on Thursday," the Chief of Staff ended.

"Good. What in God's name was that Grady idiot doing at the luncheon?" Buehler asked.

"#1 requested that he be kept in the loop," Sullivan answered.

"Do you think he could be a problem?" Buehler asked.

"On the contrary, I was going to get your opinion on possibly recruiting him," Sullivan said. Buehler smiled and lifted his glass of scotch,

"Very good, Tom. Very good."

Assistant Chief of Staff, Grady hung up the phone. The Treasury Department would neither confirm, nor deny, their involvement in the events surrounding the kidnaping in Austin. He heard the President's helicopter land at 10:43 p.m., he was returning from a fund raiser in Pittsburgh. Grady was not at all comfortable with the events that took place at the lunch meeting, even at his tender political age he had seen scams that could destroy an opponent or catapult a candidate. The thought of a large, well-orchestrated conspiracy returned to his mind. Grady could understand Buehler's role, but was baffled by the prospect of Chief of Staff Sullivan being involved. 'He has to be, too many coincidences, acting out of character and breaking the chain of command. But why?' the young Chief of Staff asked himself. There was a light knock on his office door.

"Yes?" Grady yelled.

"May I come in?" The President asked, as he opened the door. Grady quickly jumped to his feet,

"Of course, sir." The President entered and shut the door behind him. He sat in the standard issue chair in front of Grady's desk and loosened his tie.

"You know Sullivan's appointment was a political favor, he was not my first choice for Chief of Staff. The party applied a great deal of pressure for him to be appointed to that position, I wanted to make him Secretary of Defense." Grady nodded, giving the impression he knew what the President was talking about. "Ellis, deep in your gut, what do you think about this Galahad situation?" #1 asked.

"Well, sir, I think you are in a tough position. Mr. Buehler's idea does have some credence to resolve the matter," Ellis replied.

"Yes, it does, and it keeps the administration from being charged with obstruction of justice," the President stated. "But Galahad is a national hero, and a killer that the United States Government trained, paid, and hired. I think he's getting screwed."

"That goes with the territory of his chosen career, sir," Grady answered evenly.

"Oh, I know that. Galahad is probably getting what he deserves, but I cannot help feeling as if I'm being handled," #1 stated. Grady sat quietly, not wanting to say anything that may be misconstrued. "As the President, I want to know your gut feeling." Grady's eyes were having a hard time meeting #1's.

"I don't know. . ." Grady decided to go for broke, he jumped out of his chair and grabbed his brief case from atop the small credenza. "Mr. President, my gut tells me there's a conspiracy going on." He showed the President the time line of events he repeatedly scrutinized. "Things just happened too fast. The Treasury acted as if they knew where the kidnappers and Galahad were going before they did. And Mr. Buehler's solution is too neat." Grady ended.

"And of course you can prove all this?" #1 said, with a smile.

"No, sir, but you asked me for my gut feeling," Grady replied. The President looked at Grady as if he were sizing him up for a job.

"The legal and prudent way to handle this situation is exactly how Buehler advised, I've already discussed it with my counsel and the Attorney General; but I agree something is not right. There are many slips from the cup to the lips, and if this scenario should go bad, you will be my Lancelot. I will not burden you now with the how's and the why's, but you'll know when, and I'll provide you with instructions how to play the knight in shining armor."

"Yes, sir," Grady said. "This is confidential between you and I, right sir?"

"No one will know that this conversation took place unless it's needed to keep the wolves at bay," #1 replied, "and I'm pretty certain Galahad is not the wolf." After #1 left Grady's office he reflected upon their conversation. His fear of being the fall guy diminished, and he was relieved that he was not the only person who thought there was something rotten in Denmark.

17

Roger's private charter landed at B.W.I. Airport shortly after 11:00 p.m. Monday night. He slipped into a disguise during the flight, and went directly to the car rental counter after deplaning and leased a Ford Taurus. Roger noticed a man and woman, trying their best not to look conspicuous, while he was at the rental counter and let the twosome follow him onto the highway. At the halfway point between Baltimore and Washington, Roger pulled into another car rental agency, changed disguises, and picked up a light-colored Subaru. On the outskirts of D.C., Roger again changed cars and discarded his disguise, as easily as he dismissed the twosome who tried to follow him. Settling into a dark New Yorker with baggage in hand, Roger headed for the Chevy Chase home of the D.C. power-broker, Charles Buehler. His Victorian estate was built in the picturesque Maryland hills, on almost 50 acres of woodland. Roger had been to Buehler's estate a few times as Galahad, and he remembered the house could not be seen from the narrow, winding road that led to a dead end just past his driveway. Roger entered the grounds, certain he had escaped detection by the alarm system. He weaved back and forth to avoid being picked up by the surveillance cameras, and used a spook device to alert him to the location of infra-red scanning systems and radio frequency movement panels. He cut away a circle of glass in the back door, just large enough to reach in and set a contact to avoid tripping the alarm. What Roger did not know was that cutting the glass had already set off the low-voltage alarm. As he closed the door behind him, the lights suddenly flashed on. Roger found himself in Buehler's mud room facing two well-dressed men and two sub-machine guns. "Good morning, Mr. Galahad, Mr. Buehler has been expecting you." Neither man frisked Roger before escorting him to the library.

Charles Buehler was sitting next to his 18th century stone fireplace in an overstuffed leather-bound chair. His butler was setting the table in front of him with some tea sandwiches and a two bottles of Glenfitisch. A matching chair sat on the other side of the table.

"All of you leave the estate," Buehler ordered.

"Sir?" One of the two suits said, implying his guest could be dangerous.

"Go on, don't worry about me, I have Galahad to protect me. You did leave Mr. Galahad with all his toys?"

"We did not search him, as you ordered," the other suit replied.

"Good, then all of you be gone," Buehler ordered, and waved his hand. Buehler and Galahad were alone in the library when the grandfather clock beside the door struck two bells. "Come sit Joe, we'll have a chit-chat." Buehler motioned for Roger to sit in the other overstuffed chair. Knowing he had been had, Roger took the chair. "I understand scotch is still your drink of choice, why don't you pour us a four finger drink and I'll explain the rules of our little reunion," Buehler said, showing his aged, yellow teeth through a broad smile. Roger poured the scotch over ice and listened. "The first and paramount rule is that if you make any move to harm me I'll simply swallow this." Buehler held up a capsule, Roger knew exactly what it was for. "I am terminally ill, all types of cancer. If you want to kill me, that's fine, I only have a few months anyway; but, I am determined not to suffer in my death. Hell, I've even hired a Kvorkian wanna-be for when the pain gets to be too much," Buehler said, quite pleased with himself.

"Why didn't you have them search me?" Roger asked.

"Simple, Galahad, after our little pow-wow you will see killing me has nothing to do with anything. Have a sandwich if you like, they're not poisoned." Buehler laughed. "Come to think of it, that's the only rule I have for our conversation," Buehler said brightly.

"Was my daughter the original target of the kidnappers?"

"Right to the point I see," Buehler said, smiling. "Yes."

"And my wife?" Roger asked, in the cold voice of Galahad.

"She was supposed to be terminated," Buehler stated, matter of factly. Buehler's reply infuriated Roger, whose response almost took him across the table. Seeing Buehler bring the capsule dangerously near his mouth, Roger pulled back. "Oh get off your high horse! Your wife surviving gave you a 12 hour head start and we had to make adjustments," Buehler said. "Ah, the famous Galahad glare. Oh, how you must want to kill me! And how easily you forget how many wives and husbands and children you terminated. Don't you like the other shoe?" Buehler goaded, seeing Roger had settled back in his chair. "You know, Galahad, if this had been your mission it would have saved us a lot of headaches. Outside of the Mesad, you just can't get good spooks like you and Carlos anymore." Roger ignored Buehler's commentary.

"Why? The agreement we had was still in place."

"Oh, the whys of the world. Joe, see if you can understand this," Buehler pleaded, patronizing him. "If you had died a natural death, or if we had you killed, which, by the way, was many of our people's first choice, the information you possess still may have come to the surface. It was decided, or should I say I decided, it would be better to discredit you; that way if the information does leak out, it will not be nearly as damaging," Buehler explained.

"Discredit me?" Roger asked, confused.

"Well, tomorrow the President and FBI will announce the amazing story of Roger Brown's heroic rescue of his daughter. Every American will be ecstatic about the safe return of your child, but the President will order a complete investigation by the Justice Department. On Wednesday or Thursday, the Justice Department will issue a warrant for your arrest, citing vigilantism is illegal. I am confident your Jew lawyer will have you acquitted on the basis of justifiable homicide. In fact, you'll become something of a national hero." Buehler paused and took a sip of his drink. "During the course of the trial, which will certainly draw its fair share of media attention, some aggressive reporters will do your bio. You know as well as I do that they will only be able to go back seven years, causing even more intrigue. Buehler smiled and took another sip of his scotch. Theatrically, with his arms moving like an orchestra conductor, he continued, "We will fight, all the way to the Supreme Court, that your previous life is privileged information and has no bearing whatsoever on the trial at hand. Of course we will win, and even if we were to lose, we would win. Thanks to your diligent work, there is no connection from Roger Brown, to Galahad, to Joe Wilson. I guess I am the only person alive that can positively affirm that Joe Wilson, Roger Brown and Galahad are one in the same.

"How will this discredit me?" Roger asked.

"Well, if the court does order the Roger Brown witness protection program files unsealed, they will be shocked to learn that Roger Brown was formerly Vladimir Stoichi, a former KGB officer who defected at the same time Galahad disappeared. The intelligence community won't be able to discern whether Galahad is Stoichi, or a double agent," Buehler replied.

"And if the courts do not open the files?"

"Oh, that's easy too, we just slip enough information through to the media to ensure that you are marked as a KGB officer who defected."

"Why? Is the information I have all that damaging?" Galahad asked. Buehler began to laugh hysterically.

"For being the best spook ever, your naivete is amazing." Roger tried to think what he could have stolen that was so threatening. "Let me ask you something, Joe," Buehler said, flashing his yellow teeth again. "What is it you think you have?" Roger, seeing no point in holding out, answered,

"Some files on United States intelligence agents, and a few computer discs of SR-71 surveillance."

"You really don't know, do you?" Buehler asked.

"Know what?" Roger countered.

"Well, hell, my boy, there's nothing you can do now if you know the truth, so I might as well tell you. Sit back and I'll let you in on one of the biggest secrets of mankind," Buehler gloated.

"Over 50 years ago, at the end of World War II, I was involved in U.S. intelligence. I had just turned 40. When Russia and the other allies met in Berlin, a few of us foresaw great opportunity for wealth and power. Not the power a president or prime minister is perceived to have, but real power. A dozen of us formed an alliance, from Asia, to Europe, to North and South America. Our purpose was to discretely help one anothers' causes, without questioning motive. As the years went by our Alliance grew in number and power. Along the way we had what you would call a casualty or two, mostly due to poor recruiting, but by the early 1950's we could reach any place on earth. McCarthyism just happened to fit into our plans, as did having Kennedy elected. Nixon actually won in 1960, you know, but a few tweeks of a few districts in Chicago turned it toward Kennedy. The space program also made billions for our organization. In early 1963 one of the original members wanted Kennedy removed. He did not say so in so many words, but his request made his intentions obvious." Buelher stopped and reflected a moment before he continued. "The Oliver Stone movie was the closest report of the truth, not his conspiracy plot, but the theory of how black-op assassiniations could be completed. No one person knew when and who, each member of the Alliance just carried out his small part with blinders on until the big picture came into focus. The implication of the CIA, and LBJ, and the mob, as Stone portrayed, was all rubbish; and Kennedy was not killed because of Vietnam either. A few members of Kennedy's party who were loyal to Hoover, and really didn't like the boys from Boston, helped with plausible deniabliity. Their pay off was a big IOU," Buehler said, signaling Roger to refill his glass. "I guess you're wondering who killed Kennedy." Roger did not respond. "Well, the actual killer, or should I say the person who took the famous frontal shot, was your old pal, Carlos."

"I should have killed him," Roger said.

"Then I would not have come up with the idea to discredit you, as you did the Jackal," Buehler said, with a smile. "If the truth be known, JFK was killed over a woman he engaged in sex with in 1962. A jealous member of the Alliance wanted revenge, and it just so happened that a lot of people who were indebted to the Alliance, for one reason or another, wanted him dead too," Buehler finished.

"What's this have to do with me?" Roger asked.

"In due time, my boy, in due time. The Alliance had very little to do with the cover up, I still don't know why Oswald was killed. Hell, the Alliance kept the conspiracy alive by giving Garrison, the New Orleans prosecutor, most of his information to keep the fire burning. Notwithstanding, the majority of American people do not believe the single bullet theory; however, I think they would be very disconcerted to learn that their beloved President was really assassinated for having his cock in the wrong place," Buehler said, laughing.

"Get to the point," Roger ordered.

"You watch your tone," Buehler snapped back. "If you know me, then you know this is pertinent to your situation, or I would not be discussing it with you," Buehler scolded. "Now, where was I, JFK dead, Vietnam, the space race to the moon, civil rights, the women's movement, LSD, grass, oil, falling governments. . . , all devices the Alliance used to become more powerful. We knew if we could guide and divide the great American people, there was no stopping us. Hell, even spy novelists were writing about how the Alliance operated. We've only had a few summits over the years to discuss long-term strategies, always trying to look five to ten years down the road. In '66 we decided it was Nixon's time, knowing he would end the Vietnam War, so once again we positioned ourselves. What we did not know was that he had the desire to end the second Cold War as well. Hell, we milked the cold war with the Soviets for everything it was worth; and you, my friend, helped us end it when we wanted to. I'll give your regards to Gorbachev next time I see him," Buehler ended, with another haunting laugh. "But Tricky Dicky had other plans for our second Cold War with the Chinese. The members of the Democratic Party, who had helped the Alliance by playing their part in the master plan to do away with Kennedy, called in their IOU on Nixon. They did not like how friendly Nixon was toward China, or how amiable China was toward Nixon. Nixon, I remind you, was brilliant and sparkled in foreign affairs. He was forever able to find a middle ground without compromise, and that meant the end of kickbacks from military contracts for the Democrats, and some Republicans. To be frank with you, the Alliance did not care what Nixon did, or should I say the majority of us didn't; but, as history would have it, the Democrats wanted him out and we agreed to help. The assassination of character was my idea," Buehler touted, proudly. "We had the entire Watergate scandal planned and followed it to a tee, making only minor adjustments when necessary. It worked perfectly; hell, I even got to play deep throat," Buehler said, smacking his knee at his comment. "Oh, but Nixon was smart, he figured out he was being set up. He knew of the Alliance and when it was mutually beneficial we worked together with Tricky Dicky. He turned an original member of our coalition and got him to give up the names of other Alliance members - and times and dates associated with the Kennedy assassination. He applied pressure and secured the true identities of the people who were involved with the Watergate sting." Buehler was starting to feel the effects of the scotch and looked for a response from Galahad. "He had us by the balls! We thought for sure he was going to expose all of us; and then he resigned, out of nowhere, he resigned. Nixon realized if he exposed us it would destroy the country, so, the ironic reality is that Nixon was probably the biggest hero of the 20th century. You killed the Alliance member who double crossed us in 1979 on one of your missions," Buehler smiled. "Our contacts informed us that Nixon had a computer software whiz transfer all the information onto a disc. He had names, dates and operations that would unequivocally rock the government and harm many high ranking officials. We accessed a copy of the disc and knew we had to secure the original when we saw its contents. But old Tricky Dicky hid the disc in the last place we would have ever looked, the CIA archives under SR-71 surveillance. From what I understand, and I don't claim to be a computer genius, the SR-71 surveillance information covers the real information on the disc, an art that was 20 years ahead of its time. However, today, thanks to Billy Gates and the computer generation, I am told an eight year old could obliterate the masking. We didn't learn the location of the original disc until after Nixon's death, then we discovered it was one of the discs you stole, my boy,"

Roger gulped his scotch, not knowing whether to believe the old man who was a renowned user of people. As a spook, Roger had his own opinions on how the United States Government worked and what part it played in controlling world markets. He was not as naive as the old, dying man suggested. Roger was of the opinion that different countries co-existed out of necessity, and each was a puppet on a string. At the moment, Roger felt like the dumbest puppet of all, not the best counter-intelligence agent in history or Congressional Medal of Honor winning Green Beret.

"What if I give you the disc back?" Roger asked, in the words of a beaten man.

"My, my, Galahad is giving up," Buehler rejoiced, "but it's too late. Can't undo what is already done, and besides, you could have made copies." Roger recovered his emotional balance and asked,

"Day was involved in this?"

"Yes, and many more. Many people very close to the top, but not the top himself," Buehler added, realizing he may have had too much to drink.

"Why Day?" Roger asked.

"We all have our reasons. I can tell you Day's motives had nothing to do with you personally, they were a result of an order for his unit stand down in November of 1963, and a cover up as a senior Senator from Texas. The one close to the top was a young, enthusiastic bureaucrat in immigration, who provided friends of the Alliance access into the United States in November of 1963." Buehler's mood suddenly changed as he thought he said too much. "Damn this disease, moments of rambling and blackouts. You were my most talented adversary, Galahad, but I got you, and I can die a happy man now, you son of a bitch," Buehler said, losing his temper. "Now get the hell out of here! I got what I wanted, I extinguished the indestructible glare in your eyes," Buehler said, motioning for him to leave. Roger rose from the chair and walked toward the door. He stopped before the grandfather clock and turned back to Buehler.

"Do me a favor, old man."

"What? Hands off your wife and kid?" Buehler barked. "Come here." Roger walked back to the old man's chair and the dying power broker handed him an attache case containing over 200 photographs of Roger's rescue of Tris. The last few showed an ambulance at the property line of his ranch and him carrying Tris into the rear entrance of the main house. Roger felt nothing, he expected it. "I don't give a fuck if they live or die, Galahad. I have you by the balls, so go home to your wife and explain how you killed women and children!" Buehler shrieked.

"Mostly at your command," Roger reminded him, softly. "Do me a favor for saving your life in 'Nam."

"What," Buehler snapped.

"Promise me you won't die until after the trial." Roger tossed the photographs carelessly into the air and left the room to the sound of the old man screaming.

Roger's head was spinning as he left Buehler's Maryland estate. He was on cruise control as he headed for the Four Season's Hotel in the city of brotherly love. It was not that he didn't believe the former ambassador, nor was it the fathomless tentacles of the Alliance that had the former spook spooked. Deep in his soul Roger knew the Apostles, the Ten, the Alliance, or whatever they called themselves, controlled many of the events in the latter part of the 20th century; but the realization of the Gospel according to Buehler, the reality that the world was a puppet on a string for evil, self-serving assholes like him, was disturbing. 'What do I know about Charles Buehler?' Roger asked himself, checking the speedometer as he drove north on I-95. The obvious spoke for itself, Director of the CIA, involvement with the NSA, the ambassadorship; but, what about Buehler the man? That's where Roger knew he was behind the eight ball. 'Fuck, I should know something personal about a man who's life I saved and worked with for over 20 years!' Roger said, more frustrated than angry. The only fact he knew for sure was that Buehler was something of a spook in his younger day, but quickly became a 'manager of spooks' and formed the Alliance.   He was always polite and charming, dressed in the fashion of a gentleman farmer, and carried himself with an aristocratic demeanor. Roger never heard him speak of his family, or a woman, but he had never heard any rumors of homosexuality either. He recalled Buehler liked sporting events, or, perhaps they were just a convenient place for his meetings. What was his motivation? Money? Control? Power? Roger surmised power, but if it was the climactic crescendo of power, why didn't Buehler wield it publicly.   As he passed the sign welcoming him to Philadelphia, it dawned on him that the egotistical bastard got his rocks off by running the show with the anonymity of a Mafia Don. 'That has to be it,' Roger thought. 'Regardless of the outcome, he's already assured himself a draw, if not a win."

18

Roger arrived at the Four Seasons Hotel in Center City Philadelphia at 7:14 a.m. on Tuesday morning. He unpacked his bags and ordered scrambled eggs, sausage, toast, juice and coffee from the five-star hotel's room service menu. He sat down at the antique desk, moved the monogrammed stationary and pen to the side, and pulled the phone to the center of the blotter. He dialed his ranch and reached his housekeeper, who promptly retrieved his wife. Roger asked Cat how she and Tris were doing and then spoke sweet nothings to his lover. Before hanging up Cat asked,

"Rog, is everything going to be alright?"

"There may be some bumpy roads ahead, and we may want to consider the possibility of relocating, but the three of us will be fine," Roger reassured her.

"When do you think you'll be coming home?" Cat asked.

"Probably late today or early tomorrow, I only have one other person to speak with." They again pledged their undying love to one another and hung up. Within seconds of replacing the receiver in its cradle there was a knock on the door. The steward set the tray on top of the coffee table in front of the TV and Roger tipped him five dollars. He gulped the food down in under three minutes and returned to the antique desk with his second cup of coffee. Roger dialed the home number of Irving Stein at 8:21 a.m. The housekeeper informed Roger that Mr. Stein already left for the office, and provided him with the number for his cell phone. Roger thanked her, quickly disconnected the line, and anxiously dialed the cell phone number, his fingers fumbling over the buttons. Roger knew the

131

old man and the Alliance backed him in a corner, and he only had one opportunity to save his family from the embarrassment of being ostracized by the United States Government. On his second attempt, he reached his long time attorney.

"Hello?" Stein answered.

"Irving, it's Roger."

"I noticed your spot stopped running around midnight last night," Stein stated.

"Yes, but there's been a few very important developments since then. I need to see you ASAP," Roger said.

"When do you want to meet?" Stein asked.

"In an hour or two," Roger replied.

"Fine, meet me at my office at One Logan Square at 10:00 a.m."

Roger contacted the concierge desk and learned it would only take ten minutes to reach One Logan Square via taxi. He provided the clerk with his credit card number and instructed her to secure a limousine for him for 24 hours, and have it waiting out front at 9:30 a.m. Roger made a mental note to give the concierge a C note for her help. He finished his coffee, showered, shaved and dressed in a dark blue suit with a white shirt and burgundy tie. He laced up his Bostonian wing tips, picked up his brief case and room key, and proceeded to the lobby. He introduced himself to the concierge and a black stretch limo appeared in seconds. Roger thanked the attentive amanuensis and slipped the C note into her hand. The driver delivered Roger to One Logan Square in eight minutes. He exited the car and ordered his chauffeur to wait, indicating he may be a while.

Roger promenaded through the tall, revolving glass doors of the refurbished Philadelphia skyscraper. He located Stein's firm on the directory and proceeded to the 46th floor. Roger gave his name to the receptionist and was immediately escorted to Stein's office. The two men had not seen one another for seven years and Stein commented that the interlude since Roger's retirement treated him well. Roger's suit accentuated his deep, dark blue eyes, the touch of gray at his temples gave him an aristocratic flair, and the extra weight he put on showed a man who was living a life of contentment. He was initially taken back by Stein's appearance. Only a few years his senior, Stein had the halo of a man who was losing his hair and an untrimmed mustache. He wore dark, heavy rimmed glasses on his nose and looked thinner than Roger remembered. His office was very modest, considering his position in the world order, devoid of any citations of wealth. A 19th century French oak desk sat caddy corner to a window, with a view of William Penn only a few feet away. The desk was bare with only a phone and a blotter on its polished wood surface, and a single chair sat in front of it. The men shook hands and got right to the point.

"What's your status?" Stein asked, implying it must be important for the two men to meet in person.

"I've been set up by an organization called the Alliance," Roger replied. Stein raised an eyebrow as Roger continued. "The kidnaping had nothing to do with former Vice President Day's granddaughter, my daughter was the original target," Roger proclaimed.

"Go on," Stein encouraged.

"They intended for me to go after my daughter and kill the kidnappers."

"And you succeeded in all aspects I gather?"

"Yes, my daughter is fine and the kidnappers are dead. I was handled. The people of the Alliance knew I would react the way I did and now aim to discredit me, so if the information I have on them ever surfaces it will not be taken seriously."

"How do they plan to discredit you?"

"It will be announced today that my daughter has been safely returned. It will also be announced that the Justice Department is launching an investigation of the events surrounding her rescue. As the plan goes, they will charge me with vigilantism and you will get me off on justifiable homicide. During the trial it will be leaked that I am in the witness protection program. After some court battles over that issue, it will be leaked that I defected from the Soviet Union seven years ago, and my true identity is Vladimir Stoichi, a former KGB agent. The Alliance will have cast a shadow of doubt over any evidence I present against them," Roger finished.

133

"So, whatever you have on the Alliance would not be credible," Stein stated.

"So, what do we do now counsel?" Roger asked. Stein sat back in his chair and turned to the window. He removed a white, plastic ashtray from one of the drawers of the old oak desk and reached for a cigarette. He put his head back and blew little white smoke rings into the air.

"How can you be certain that I am not a member of this so called Alliance?" Stein asked. Roger was shocked by the question and completely taken off guard.

"A few reasons," Roger said, not wanting to show Stein he was starting to get suspicious.

"The Alliance, that's what they call themselves these days," Stein remarked. "Some people refer to them as 'The Ten' or 'The Apostles.' You of all people had to know of their existence," Stein ended. Roger was beginning to feel very uncomfortable from the conversation and the small chair he was sitting in. He figured the latter was intentional, but he was unsure about the conversation.

"Of course I've heard of a group of people who were the power behind the power," Roger answered.

"But never really believed it?" Stein questioned.

"Not that, I just didn't know they were so well organized," Roger answered.

"How do you know how organized they are?" Roger was tiring of the verbal tennis match and responded to Stein in the harsh voice of Galahad,

"I have my methods."

"But you still have not answered my question, how can you be sure that I am not a member of the Alliance?" Stein toyed. Roger was beginning to feel the effects of no sleep and loosened his tie.

"For one, when I gave you the information on the Swiss banks. If you were a member, there would have been no restitution for the holocaust victims," Roger blurted out.

"That's it?" Stein asked, as he exhaled and put his cigarette out.

"Two, if I believed you were one of them, you would be dead now," Roger said evenly, looking through Stein's thick, brown-rimmed glasses.

"You said there were a few reasons, what else?" Stein pressed.

"Buehler all but told me you weren't at his victory party."

"Charles Buehler," Stein repeated.

"Well, are you?" Roger asked. There was a long silence.

"To be good, one must have bad; to be happy, one has to know sadness. Being good and being happy are a result of your perception of certain events. No, I am not a member of the Alliance, they would probably consider me their competition."

"I'm glad to hear that, I did not want to kill you." Both men laughed.

"When did Buehler tell you about me?" Stein asked.

"Everything I've told you in regard to my circumstances, and his love for you, was explained to me early this morning at his estate in Chevy Chase," Roger said.

"You saw through the set up?' Stein asked.

"I guess," Roger answered.

"It's a shame you can't prove your conversation," Stein said.

"Why is that?" Roger asked.

"Then we might have been able to apply some pressure to relieve some pressure," Stein explained.

"Funny you should mention that. He knew I was coming and had two gorillas in suits armed with machine guns waiting for me, but they escorted me to him without searching me. He taunted me to kill him, claiming he was terminally ill." Stein shrugged his shoulders,

"So?" Roger tossed a small cassette tape on the 19th century desk.

"That's one of three copies of our conversation. Stein retrieved a small tape recorder and headphones from another room and listened to the tape. When he finished he said,

"Oh, by the way, D.C. has announced the return of your daughter, followed by the announcement of a Justice Department inquiry."

"Where do we go from here?" Roger asked.

"To lunch," Stein answered, as he picked up the phone and told his secretary what to order. "Do you care for anything now?" he asked, as he excused himself from the office.

"Coffee would be great," Roger replied. A young lady in her twenties, with dark hair and dark eyes, set a carafe of coffee and two cups on the oak desk. While Roger was working on his second cup, the young lady returned with a large brown bag containing two cheese steaks. Roger tried one of the Philadelphia delicacies the last time he was in the city and decided it was the roll that made the sandwich. Stein returned to the modest office an hour and twenty minutes later to find that Brown had consumed both sandwiches and soft drinks, and was napping in the large chair behind the desk. Stein cleared his throat.

"I'm not asleep, counselor, what's up?" Stein sat in the small chair in front of the desk and realized how uncomfortable it must have been for the much larger Brown.

"My mother country, Israel, would have as much to lose as the United States if this type of information was ever to surface," Stein stated.

"So, you want me to go along with the set up?" Roger asked.

"No, I didn't say that," Stein rebutted. "Without a strong U.S., Israel would be run amuck by our Arab friends. I'm sure you have a good understanding of global relations 101." Roger tapped his finger on the desk and glanced at his watch. It was 1:05 p.m., he had been in Stein's office for almost four hours.

"So, Israel wants assurance that I'll never use the disc for the good of the world," Roger stated.

"No, not Israel," Stein answered, "I want assurance."

"I don't understand."

"My contacts have always suspected the Alliance, as you have come to know it, had its tentacles in a lot of areas it shouldn't. We did know Oswald was not Kennedy's killer, we always believed it was the conservatives of this country. Watergate, the Iran Contra Affair, the overthrow of some other governments. . . . We always suspected, but we never, how did you put it, 'think they were so organized.' Well, we don't think it's as bad as it appears."

"So, you want me to take the fall," Roger restated.

"Partially, but not a total fall. My people have no idea who I'm dealing with. I grant you they always suspected that I knew where you were, and trust me, I've used that to my advantage more times than I can remember. You would be amazed how dropping a line like 'perhaps I'll have my friend visit you' can turn the tables during contractual negotiations. I assure you the announcement that Galahad made a comeback this week was no great revelation, I've kept you alive and very well in Asia, Europe, and especially the Middle East, under another alias of course. When the Langley boys did not open their mouths, I knew you had destroyed everything connecting you to Galahad. Since perception is 90% of reality, I've been Galahad the last five years or so, if not by name, definitely by action. So, you see, Mr. Brown, this is a little more complicated than it appears," Stein concluded.

"You and yours are just as fucking bad as the Alliance," Brown said, as he rose from Stein's chair behind the old oak desk. "The fees I've paid you were probably crumbs compared to the amount of money you made pretending to be me. No wonder you've always shown me such complaisance," Roger ended.

"Something like that," Stein said. "There still may be a way to find some middle ground."

"Oh, yeah? Like what?" Roger snapped.

"You must trust me completely," Stein said.

"Why should I?" Roger countered.

"Because unless you want to be the fall guy and be known as a KGB defector for the rest of your life, which Buehler knows would drive the Medal of Honor Winning Green Beret in you absolutely crazy, you really have no choice," Stein said. "I will need the disc and the tapes, and in return I give you this." Stein handed Roger a manilla envelope with three passports, a few bank cards, and a slip of paper containing the password to a seven digit Swiss account. "There's over a billion dollars in that Swiss account, the passports are for Joe Wilson, Patricia Wilson and Cathy Wilson of the United States. You know how to use the passports and money to relocate to any place in the world. I will liquidate all your assets and deposit the money slowly into your Swiss account, that's close to another $800 million - and this is only if things go wrong. But as I said before, I'll need the disc."

"Why all the emphasis on the disc? You're making me wonder if you and the Mesad are part of the master plan," Roger said, taking off his jacket and exposing the Glock.

"It will be needed to finalize the deal," Stein replied.

"I see, run it down for me," Roger instructed.

"My objective is to make certain the United States is not subject to leaks that would weaken the government, which in turn would put my country in grave danger. I want the President and the administration to be aware that there's a bad apple on the top of the basket. With him exposed, the Alliance will be set back a few years. For these insights, I will request the U.S. Justice Department have a swift trial of Roger Brown, and have the White House make a public statement that Mr. Brown's witness protection program files will remain sealed. It will leak out that you are a Congressional Medal of Honor recipient, but that's all anyone will know of your past," Stein ended. Roger, who was very tired, just said,

"You know the consequences."

"I know them well. Go home to your family and wait to be arrested. I'll fly to Austin when you call me and have you released on bail, but at that time I'll need the disc," Stein stated. The surety that Stein was going to complete his part of the deal first made Roger feel a little more comfortable.

"Fine," Roger said.

"One last thing, Mr. Brown, if you copied the disc, we need all copies. We can run tests that will show how many were made."

"I understand," Roger said, as he left Stein's office. He got in the limo and headed for the hotel to gather his baggage.

Roger took the first flight out of Philadelphia International Airport home to Austin.

19

Stein sat pondering the conversation he had with Brown and lit another cigarette. It was not his intention to play with Galahad emotionally, he had seen that the former spook was near the end of his rope on that account, but with the stakes so high, he had to be sure they were both on the same page. Personally, he did not care about Galahad's fate, but, once again, their objectives seemed to run in the same direction. He snubbed out his cigarette and used a secure line to inquire about the location of the Israeli Ambassador to the United States. Stein was in luck, Ambassador Harvey Glickman was in Washington, D.C. Glickman was a former import-export entrepreneur, a true middleman. He also helped the Israeli Government whenever called upon, be it arms, information, or technology. One of Glickman's most prized connections was Irving Stein. The power-broker attorney spoke with Glickman at the Israeli embassy around 4:00 p.m., and set a date for dinner at the embassy at 8:30 p.m.

Stein arrived at the embassy, in the heart of D.C., twenty minutes early. He had attended a few fund raisers there over the past ten years, and disliked the modern structure of the six bedroom mausoleum. He helped himself to a seltzer water with lemon and waited a half hour before the plump ambassador arrived. Glickman suggested they have dinner served in his study for security reasons. The two men entered the soundproof study, which was carpeted from floor to ceiling, and sat opposite one another at a modern desk. A kosher meal of Filet Mignon with Bearnaise sauce, baked potatoes, green beans almandine, fresh garden salad and chocolate mousse was delivered by one of the waitresses. Stein meticulously outlined the dilemma of Israel's Big Brother, in Hebrew, over dinner.

"Our Big Brother has himself in quite a predicament," Glickman said, as he poured himself a second cup of coffee. Stein took out of pack of cigarettes and looked to Glickman for approval. The ambassador nodded and produced a clear glass ashtray from under the desk.

"Yes, but we have several options how to handle it," Stein offered, knowing Glickman was connected to the intelligence arena.

"Perhaps we should just stay on the sidelines and let the chips fall where they may," Glickman said, sipping his coffee. "The world has changed in the past several years, people like Galahad are expendable."

"That was my first reaction this afternoon," Stein said, "but there is the potential of serious negative fallout, for Big Brother, if Galahad gets his information out. A certain percentage of the American populous is going to believe him and. . ." Stein's words trailed off.

"Your personal safety is at risk," Glickman finished. "What is he like? Galahad I mean." Stein deliberated the question while finishing his cigarette.

"He still has the air of confidence that he always had, and is still probably very dangerous as an intelligence agent; but, in the same respect, he is only a shadow of his former self. Galahad has liabilities now, he has a family."

"I see. What do you think we should do with our new found information?" Glickman asked.

"Choose the lesser of two evils," Stein proclaimed. "Could you arrange a meeting with the President for tomorrow?"

"I'm sure I could get a ten minute audience, he's always very accommodating to the Jews," Glickman said, with a smirk.

"Let's listen to the tape," Stein said, as he produced a tape recorder from his brief case.

"Who do you think the high ranking official close to the President is?" Glickman queried. Stein rewound the tape and replaced it in his briefcase.

"I made a few inquiries before meeting with you this evening and learned that Thomas Sullivan worked for immigration from June, 1963 to February, 1964. His subsequent post was with the Democratic National Committee, at twice his former salary," Stein answered. "We already know the information on the tape, and what Galahad has may not be very specific, but we in the intelligence field have our own insights. A few years back, in the late '80's, we buried some damaging information for the Alliance regarding the Watergate scandal," Stein concluded.

"You still believe that the Alliance and the CIA are ignorant of your true function for the Israeli Government?" Glickman asked.

"Only you, the Prime Minister, and one trusted employee of the Israeli government know my true part in the world order," Stein declared curtly, implying it was not to be discussed.

"Big Brother would be very shocked and embarrassed to learn that the head of the Mesad operated out of one of its largest cities," Glickman concluded. Obviously disturbed by the statement, Stein was silent. Glickman let his words hang in the air, like a child who told his father the mail man had lunch with mommy everyday. "What is our next step?"

"Go to the President tomorrow and tell him what you know. Tell him about Sullivan and arrange for someone the President trusts to get in touch with me as soon as possible to verify the authenticity of the tape. Once things are made right for Galahad, I'll return the tapes and disc to Big Brother," Stein answered.

"I don't understand. Wouldn't you be at risk of exposing yourself?" Glickman asked. Stein lit another cigarette and scratched his head, which seemed to have less hair on it now than it did a week ago.

"I think you would agree returning the tapes and the disc to Big Brother is the prudent course of action, they do give our motherland an umbrella of security."

"Yes, I understand that. It's your personal involvement that concerns me," Glickman said, leaning forward to make his point.

"The Alliance and Big Brother already know I have links to Galahad, it would draw more attention my way if I didn't help him. And the fact that I know this will weaken the Alliance does wonders for my soul! I'm sure you agree that we don't want Big Brother to become aware that I handled their #1 spook for 15 years," Stein explained, patiently.

"I see," Glickman said, "all but the part about handling Galahad."

"I usually had a good idea where he was, and with a little deduction, and some good work by our own intelligence department, I usually knew what Big Brother was up to, too. If it was in our interest, I would act accordingly," Stein said.

"And the Alliance thought we had someone deep in their camps," Glickman stated.

"We did. Do you remember Saul Fox?" Stein asked.

"Yes, a banker in New York. Died in a car accident about 20 years ago," Stein replied.

"That was the member of the Alliance that Nixon turned and Galahad killed, as much on my order as the Alliances'. I know it's all very entwined, but the webs of the intelligence and counter-intelligence world work that way. My position in the Mesad enabled us to work very closely with the CIA and NSA, they never knew I was in charge of the Mesad, as I never knew they were in bed with the Alliance. When our interests were concurrent, operations ran very smoothly, when they did not, the first one to handle Galahad usually won, because he eliminated the competition," Stein finished.

"I see. I admit I don't fully understand the inner workings..."

"Let me put it to you another way - it's in Israel's best interest to see that Big Brother does not suffer any fall out from its indiscretions over the last 30 years."

"I understand," Glickman said.

"It is also in our country's best interest to have the Alliance weakened and have Galahad return to the deep freeze, so he does not figure out he was being handled by our government," Stein explained, tiring of his didactic discourse to the diplomat. "Tell the President that if he gets Galahad back in the deep freeze, we will give him the tapes and the disc. Stein stood up, shook Glickman's hand, and returned to Philadelphia.

Roger arrived back at his ranch at 1:00 a.m. Wednesday morning. While parking the pick-up truck, he was approached by the sergeant he left in charge.

"Any problems?" Roger asked.

"Nothing too big, only that hired hand," the sergeant replied.

"I told him to take a vacation," Roger stated.

"Well, the old geezer was too worried about the cattle to leave. We almost shot him yesterday when he was dropping bales of hay for the herd."

"Anything else?" Roger asked.

"Nah, everything's been pretty quiet."

"Gather everyone for a pow-wow at 12:00 p.m., Roger ordered.

"Yes, sir," the sergeant answered.

"Good night." Roger climbed the stairs to the master bedroom and stopped in to kiss Tris.

"Hi Daddy," Tris said, surprising her father.

"Hi there, princess. You should be asleep," Roger said.

"I was until you woke me up," the four year-old replied. Roger fluffed the covers and re-tucked her in, trying not to show how desperately tired he was.

"Good night, sweetheart." He left her room and headed for his wife and his bed.

Cat was sitting up in bed wearing a sheer night gown. Her hair had been washed and Roger noticed the bandage covering her chest wound was smaller.

"Hi Cat," Roger said, with as much enthusiasm as he could muster, as he walked over and gave her a kiss.

"Hi," Cat answered, as she kissed and hugged her husband. "How did things go?"

"Well, I think things might just work out for the three of us," Roger said. Cat saw the pure exhaustion on her husband's face.

"Then that's all that matters. Come get in bed, you need a good night's rest."

"I'm so tired, too tired for rest," Roger said, stripping down to his skivvies and climbing in the large, king size bed. Cat turned off the light and Roger felt her curl up next to him, resting her head on his shoulder. Roger took a deep breath and let out a sigh. He felt Cat's fingers dance over his chest and stomach, and underneath his underwear. Roger grabbed her hand and said,

"They'll be plenty of time for that when you heal up." Cat reflected back to her days of turning tricks and ignored her husbands objections. The climax for Roger was quick, intensified by the days events and lack of energy in his body. Sleep came quickly.

Grady could not get the conversation with #1 out of his mind. As he returned from the men's room, he saw Israeli Ambassador, Glickman leaving the west wing of the White House. He did not recall any visits scheduled from the Israeli embassy on #1's agenda. When he reached his office the message light on his phone was lit. Grady entered his password and retrieved the communique from #1's secretary, 'Mr. Grady, the President would like to see you at once. He instructed me to inform you not, and I repeat, not, to let *anyone* know you are coming to see him.' The clock on his phone read Wednesday, 10:38 a.m.

The President was standing by the window, observing the greens of summer turning to the golds of fall, when Grady was announced. The President returned to his desk and pressed the panel button to stop all recording devices.

"Ellis, come, sit," #1 said, as he sat down in his comfortable chair behind the first desk. The feeling of being the fall guy was rising once again in his gut. "Does anyone know you're here?"

"Only your secretary," Grady answered.

"Mr. Sullivan?" the President inquired.

"He's at the Justice Building today. No one knows I'm here except for you, your secretary and the secret service men who let me in," Grady assured the President.

"You still up for a little job?" #1 asked.

"Yes sir, I just hope it's not illegal," Grady replied.

"Would that make a difference?" #1 asked.

"No, but I just don't want to be the one holding the bag," Grady said. The President smiled.

"I want you to go to Philadelphia and listen to a tape that a man by the name of Irving Stein has in connection to the Galahad situation. Listen, take note of its authenticity, and report back to me ASAP." The President handed Grady a slip of paper with Stein's name and phone number on it.

"That's it?" Grady asked.

"Don't call him until you get to Philly, and please try not to let anyone know your whereabouts," #1 finished. He shook Grady's hand over the desk and walked him to the door. "It's 11:30 a.m., you should be back around 6:00 p.m.; come straight to my office when you return. God speed."

Grady drove his Chevrolet north on I-95. He was hyperventilating, his palms were sweating, and he had a severe case of paranoia. 'Fuck, I'm not cut out for this cloak and dagger shit, I'm an administrator!' Grady yelled to himself, checking his rear view mirror for the hundredth time. Traveling through the Harbor tunnel beneath the Chesapeake, he thought, 'Great, I don't know who I'm going to meet or what it's for. For all I know Galahad could be waiting there to make me another notch on his belt.' It was 2:20 p.m. when Grady parked his car in a secure lot at 30th Street Station and located a pay phone. 'I just can't say the President of the United States told me to call,' Grady thought, before it dawned on him that the person on the other end of the phone would already know that. "I'm in the majors now," he said, as he dialed Stein's number. After the second ring a man's recorded voice instructed him to travel via taxi to the 555 Building on City Avenue, take the elevator to the ninth floor, and proceed to Suite 902. The taxi ride from the train station took forty-five minutes due to heavy westbound traffic. The stretch of Route 1 known as City Avenue, is lined with fine stores, restaurants, and office complexes. On the east side of the highway lies Philadelphia, to the west, the gateway to one of the world's wealthiest communities, the Main Line. Grady tipped the driver and entered the building. He noticed a very attractive, dark-haired lady in the sundry shop across from the elevator bank. He smiled politely while he waited for the car, relieved no one else was around. He rode the muzakless elevator non-stop to the ninth floor, located Suite 902, and knocked on the door. A man in his early fifties, sporting dark brown glasses, introduced himself as Irving Stein.

"Mr. Grady?"

"Yes, sir," Grady replied.

"Come in, sit. Can I get you anything? Soda? Water?"

"No, I'm fine, thank you," Grady answered, sitting in the lone chair in the 6'x8' room.

"Your job is to authenticate one of the voices on this tape. You may deny the content, but don't let that interfere with your task. Stein handed Grady a set of headphones. At the conclusion of the tape Stein saw Grady's expression of disbelief. "Go report to your President." The man with the dark glasses collected the tape recorder and headphones and disappeared through a door opposite the one Grady entered. It was 7:14 p.m. Wednesday evening when Grady returned to the White House. All fears of being the fall guy succumbed to the fear of the information on the tape.

The exclusive gentleman's club was vacant. Sullivan had just finished with a new young man and was headed for the showers when John Kelley appeared.

"Hi, Tom, everything satisfactory?"

"Very nice," the Chief of Staff answered.

"I have a message for you. I don't know who it's from, but I was paid a lot of money to give it to you, 'everything as planned,'" Kelley said. "See you around, Tom, maybe we can work out together sometime."

"Maybe, see you later," Sullivan replied. The President's secretary had phoned the Chief of Staff and informed him #1 needed to see him at 8:30 p.m. after a photo session with a foreign dignitary. Sullivan thought over his visit to the Justice Department, where the lawyers were trying to put a positive spin on the Austin kidnaping. After some bickering among the Assistant District Attorneys, the Department decided to charge Brown with reckless endangerment; he would be arrested on Friday. Sullivan suggested Thursday, but the attorneys indicated they needed time to dot the I's and cross the T's. Sullivan felt good about the conspiracy, and even better about the young man who had just serviced him. He showered, dressed, and headed for the White House for his 8:30 p.m. hand-holding session with #1.

20

Roger awoke to the sight of his wife, standing in front of the full length mirror, tending to her week-old scar. Her hair was wet from the shower and her terry cloth robe had fallen to the Italian marble floor. Seeing her husband crawl out of bed, she kidded,

"I hope you can become an ass man." Roger did not comprehend Cat's comment until he was brushing his teeth and saw her reflection in the mirror. She had removed the bandage on her chest, exposing a road map of surgical scars and drain depressions. He walked over and kissed her,

"Once we get through our little problems and you heal, we'll have you fixed good as new. Roger saw it was 11:45 a.m. "I have some work to do and a few phone calls to make. Why don't we have brunch in an hour, or so, on the terrace?'

"Okay, is there anything I can do to help?" Cat asked.

"You did last night," Roger said, as he pinched his wife's rear end. "I should know more by tonight, we'll discuss everything later after Tris is in bed." Rogers instincts told him to trust Stein, he had no choice. He was confident the attorney would come through, but his gut told him it was not for the reasons they discussed in Philadelphia.

The seven Beret's were gathered in Roger's basement office when he arrived a minute after noon. He wrote each man a check for $10,000 and inquired about his personal situation. Five of the men had families and regular jobs, two were divorced, and one was unemployed. "If you're questioned by the IRS, tell them the money was a gift; that way you won't have to pay income tax on it. We'll keep the fact that you worked your asses off and put your lives on the line for it between us." He shook each man's hand and thanked him as he left, until only the one who had no job or family remained.

"You want to hang around for a while?" Roger asked.

"Don't have any other offers," the man who Roger helped with a drug problem 14 years prior stated.

"Okay, bunk with the old geezer. You get three squares a day and I'll pay you $500.00 per week as a hired hand and another $500 as security," Roger said.

"Great, colonel," the reformed addict said. "And thanks for believing in me when no one else did. I found Jesus you know."

"Good, you can pray for my soul while you work," Roger said, as he dismissed the man. He called the old hired hand and told him the beret would be staying on to help with the chores. "Fill him in on running the ranch, where and where not to go," Roger ordered. He trusted the Green Beret with his life, but he didn't want any unnecessary embarrassment.

The next item on his agenda concerned the First Bank of Austin. The events surrounding Tris' abduction overshadowed his business interests and Roger still had the profitable lease agreement in his briefcase. He faxed a copy to the bank and called his account executive to verify the transmission. He also arranged for the ranch's business income and bills to be handled by automatic draft and had the Green Beret added to the payroll.

"How much do I have with your bank?" Roger asked. The account executive, who Roger had been dealing with for five years, tapped some keys on his computer and answered,

"The corporation has $165 million, that figure includes the $100 million deposited last week."

"You have a real estate department, correct?" Roger asked.

"Yes, sir," the account executive replied.

"Discretely, and I mean very discretely, make some inquiries to sell the entire ranch; I would think the new lease agreement would make the property value skyrocket."

"Yes, it would, but trying to sell 500,000 acres and the main house might mean subdividing and real estate syndications," the account exec replied.

148

"See what you can come up with and let me know," Roger closed.

Roger removed the rug to descend to his secret office for his last set of phone calls. Stein's words kept playing over and over in his head, 'What did he mean he kept me alive for the last five years? Why would a reputable attorney do that?' Roger sat at the simple wooden table and called the Swiss bank. He identified himself as Joe Wilson, gave his seven digit identification number, and received verification that $1.1 billion was in the account. Roger ordered $100 million to be invisibly transferred to a New Zealand bank under the name of Peter Bishop. He gave the Swiss banker the New Zealand account number and asked how long the transaction would take. The banker assured him, in a thick German accent, the transfer would be completed in thirty minutes. During the wait, Roger committed the account numbers of Roger Brown of Austin, Joe Wilson of Switzerland and Peter Bishop of New Zealand to memory. He wrote the numbers down on a single sheet of paper and put them in a sealed envelope addressed to Tris. He mailed the envelope to his probate attorney in Austin, indicating it was only to be opened in the event of his death. Roger made his final call to the New Zealand National Bank. The clerk confirmed a $100 million deposit, but could not verify the source of the funds. Roger was pleased the Swiss bank did a thorough job of transferring the money invisibly. 'That's why those Swiss banks get paid the big bucks,' he said to himself. Peter Bishop was Roger's only safe house. Even Stein did not know about that alias, or the small estate on ten acres in the New Zealand hills. As he ascended the hidden stairs, Roger again thought of Stein, 'Maybe he has another agenda. I know he works with the Mesad, but to what extent?' He let the thought slip from his mind and joined Cat and Tris on the terrace and brunch.

Sullivan noticed the Secret Service detail was doubled when he approached the Oval Office. He received his clearance, knocked, and entered. Forty five minutes earlier, the President met with Grady and Attorney General, Jonathan Stanton. Stanton was a tall, slender man in his mid-50's with graying hair. Previously a law professor at Yale University, he was confirmed as the Attorney General at the beginning of the administration's second term. Stanton was considered by many of his peers to be the foremost expert on the Constitution.

"Well, Ellis, how did your meeting with Mr. Stein go?" the President asked. Grady's eyes shot quickly to the Attorney General and back to the President, seeking permission to speak with him present. "I asked Attorney General, Stanton to be here to guide us on any legal ramifications," #1 said. "I've already briefed him on the situation."

"Well, where do I start?" Grady asked.

"First, who was on the tape," #1 asked.

"A couple of bodyguards, or secret service types in the beginning. . ." the President raised his eyebrows, as if to say 'who else?'

"Supposedly Galahad, a.k.a. Joe Wilson, and, without a doubt, Charles Buehler," Grady answered.

"Are you certain it was Charles Buehler?" the Attorney General asked.

"Oh, yes, I'm certain. How about former Vice President, Day, and the other person high in your administration?" Grady asked.

"Who do you think that person is?" the President asked, as he returned to the sofa with three manilla folders. Grady hesitated, and then answered very slowly,

"The magnitude of this conspiracy is unbelievable. The only person that has access to that much information would be the Chief of Staff." The Attorney General and the President glanced at one another.

"Very good, Ellis. Very good. You do understand the delicacy with which this situation must be handled," #1 reinforced.

"I think so, but I'm not certain," Grady replied.

"A knee-jerk reaction might be as harmful as Galahad broadcasting the information on the disc over CNN," #1 explained. "Jonathan will guide us as to what we can and cannot do. The number one objective in my mind, for national security reasons, is to bury the hatchet; rewriting history would cause more harm than good. The second objective is to make the

Alliance less powerful and decrease the amount of control they have in the government, there may not be too much we can do to lessen their power in business. Third, we want to get Galahad back into the deep freeze after we get the tape, he's been through enough. And last, but not least, we need to find out what Irving Stein's real connection to the Israeli Government is. Jonathan will draw up a document stating he was consulted on all matters, and that I acted in my capacity as President in a prudent manner."

"So, whatever the fallout there can be no obstruction of justice," Grady said, rhetorically.

"I didn't ask for this bullshit to land in my lap, but by God I'm going to end it," #1 stated angrily.

"How do you know who to trust? There's no line up card to distinguish the sides," Grady said, to no one in particular. The President and the Attorney General both smiled.

"There's a lot of truth in your naivete, Ellis. That's exactly why I turned to Jonathan for help, and not the CIA or FBI. Before joining the administration he was a scholar, not an advocate or lobbyist for special interest groups. I believe the Alliance has moles in the agencies, and the sad thing is the moles probably don't even know what they're into," the President remarked. "Jonathan, why don't you explain the legal ramifications that we are challanged with in this affair." The Attorney General shuffled some papers and paced around the couch.

"My first concern is how to get Galahad through a quick trial with due process. The President cannot intervene because it would be construed as an obstruction of justice. When we arrest him on Friday, the charges will be manslaughter and reckless endangerment. To take the sting out of the impact of the charges and undermine the Alliance's plan, we'll beat them to the punch and announce that Galahad was a former Green Beret and Congressional Medal of Honor recipient who was placed in the witness protection program after a successful career as an intelligence officer. Brown has already done a thorough job of cutting all connections to his past, we simply provide him with a bridge from Green Beret to Roger Brown. We will not pursue charging Buehler, Sullivan, or former Vice President Day, with treason. . . ."

"Why not?" Grady interrupted.

"National security, son," #1 answered.

"The President will be able to resolve those situations much more effectively through political means, without breaking the law, under the realm of national security. I've already signed off on it, so there cannot be any future prosecution of anyone involved in this affair. In other words, I don't think I could get a conviction even with Galahad's evidence; a lot of key witnesses are dead and the risk just doesn't warrant the return. We get Galahad out and the President takes care of the others," Stanton concluded, still trying to talk himself into the plan.

There was a knock on the door and Chief of Staff, Thomas Sullivan entered. Grady, #1, and Stanton glanced at one another.

"Come in Tom, I need to discuss some very important matters with you," the President said as he returned to the chair behind his desk. Sullivan walked slowly to the Attorney General and greeted him with a handshake. He shot the Assistant Chief of Staff a look that unmistakenly said, 'what are you doing here?' The President took the first chair and began his systematic assault on Sullivan and the Alliance.

"Tom, do you know what these are?" #1 asked, holding up the three manilla folders.

"Yes, Mr. President, they are personal history files," Sullivan answered, trying to keep an even tone.

"Do you know whose personal history files these are?" #1 asked.

"I assure you I don't," the Chief of Staff answered.

"Let's see," the President said, as he picked up one of the files and began to read, "Charles Buehler: ambassador, CIA, NSA; interesting how a bureaucrat gathered such wealth coming from a modest background," The President commented. "Former Vice President Day: command officer in Texas, Dallas, November 1963, to be more precise." #1 looked over his glasses for a response from the Chief of Staff. "Then we come to Thomas Sullivan, let's see what we have here. Ah, in November of 1963 an immigration officer," the President said, with the dramatics of a bad actor. "Does that mean anything to you, Tom?" Sullivan looked at the President, smiled a little, and replied,

"That I worked for the Immigration Office when I was a young man." The President snapped to his feet and tossed the files across his desk, one of them carrying itself to the floor.

"Oh, get off it, Tom! Galahad has you, Buehler and Day tightly tied to the Alliance. He gave us the disc," the President bellowed.

"I assure you Mr. President, I don't have any idea what you're talking about," Sullivan replied, maintaining his composure.

"Let me tell you something, Tom, after you and Buehler handled me into coming down on Galahad to discredit him, Galahad visited the old man after the football game early Tuesday morning. Buehler's overblown ego and deteriorating health got in the way of his obsession to destroy Galahad. The old fool ordered his security men not to search him, just so he could tell Galahad how he beat him and declare his victory. The Alliance would have been home free if the old man wasn't so damn arrogant and vindictive. Buehler's little chat with Galahad included names, places and events, such as November of 1963, Watergate, and a few others. While taunting Galahad to kill him the old egotistical bastard also told him of your plan to discredit him," the President said, now pacing around the Oval Office. Sullivan turned and addressed the President with a firmer tone of voice,

"You're going to take the word of a killer over Charles Buehler's?"

"You idiot. Galahad taped the entire conversation with Buehler. I had it verified and cross checked with the disc."

"I can grant you immunity, as I did for former Vice President, Day, for your testimony," the Attorney General added. The ashen look on Sullivan's face complimented his weak words,

"You have Day?"

"He's under the faithful watch of the special forces at an undisclosed location," #1 said, with a smirk. "I'll be looking for your resignation within the half-hour."

"You have until 10:00 a.m. tomorrow morning to turn yourself in to my office," the Attorney General stated.

"One last thing, Tom," #1 said. "After you resign, I suggest you get in touch with Charles Buehler and give him this message - if we discover any media leaks regarding Galahad, we'll be arresting him too. Our doctors confirmed he'll be dead in three months, so we've decided not to go after him now, but that will change quickly, I assure you, if he decides to discredit Galahad. Sullivan left the Oval Office and returned a few minutes later with his resignation.

The sun was setting in the western sky earlier each night as October approached. Tris Brown had gone to bed with little objection after a day of splashing around in the olympic sized pool. Roger and Cat sat on the terrace, each with a flute of their favorite champagne, Dom Perignon. The alcohol and the heat of the Texas day had both perspiring, or perhaps it was the subject matter causing an adreneline rush.

"We may have to relocate," Roger said.

"Then we move," Cat answered, as she climbed slowly off her chair and layed on top of her husband on the chaise lounge.

"I don't think you understand, not just move, but leave the country and change our identity," Roger explained. Cat was nibbling at her husbands neck with kisses of promise.

"Do I get to choose your name?"

"I'm serious, Cat. I'm talking about selling the ranch, the whole nine yards," Roger said, as he ran his hand across his wife's rear and discovered she removed the bottom of her bathing suit.

"I'm serious too, fuck me," Cat answered, as she reached for her husband's groin.

"You should get shot more often," Roger answered.

Sullivan declined the President's offer of being chauffered to his home. He was assured his personal belongings would be sent to him within the week. He got in his late model Crown Victoria and the President's secret service detail escorted him off the

White House grounds. Sullivan's mind was racing as he turned left on Pennsylvania Avenue. His letter of resignation cited medical reasons, and at this moment that was the truth. He felt scared, confused, and alone, and his loveless charade of a marriage, which only included sex to produce a child, came to the forefront of his mind. He did not even know where his wife was, he was sure it was written in a daily planner in their library, but right now he was a man without a country. Sullivan found his car taking him to the Chevy Chase estate of Charles Buehler. He hit the intercom button and announced himself. After a five minute wait, the large iron gates swung open in slow motion. Sullivan entered Buehler's library and found the old man sitting in a large chair by the massive fireplace. He looked quizzically at the brilliant fire of crackling yellows, blues and whites burned beyond the hearth; the temperature outside was in the low 70's and the air conditioning was running.

"What in God's name are you doing here?" Buehler asked, without turning to acknowledge his guest.

"They have the disc," Sullivan said.

"What are you talking about?" Buehler said, turning to Sullivan with burning eyes.

"I just resigned as Chief of Staff at #1's request."

"You're telling me the President has the disc?" Buehler shouted.

"And they have Day too," the former Chief of Staff added, as he went to the bar and poured himself a whiskey.

"That's bullshit. The 12:00 news reported Day is at Fort Bragg for some reunion," Buehler replied.

"Exactly, Fort Bragg, where the Green Berets train. The President said he was being held by special forces." Sullivan emptied half his glass with one gulp, loosened his tie, and sat on the sofa.

"I don't understand, how did they get the disc?" Buehler asked.

"Through Galahad's Jew lawyer, I imagine," Sullivan said, passively.

"You imagine?" Buehler yelled. "And why the hell did you resign?"

"Because, you old egotistical fool, of your little meeting with Galahad on Tuesday morning. Galahad taped the entire fucking conversation. Hell, they knew I handled immigration in November, 1963," Sullivan said, desperately. "You couldn't have had him killed! Hell, I understand you were expecting him and ordered your security not to search him! Just to show Galahad that your intelligence was far superior to his spooks intuition! It's over."

"What about Day?" Buehler asked.

"He's already cut himself a deal," Sullivan answered.

"I don't believe it," Buehler said.

"Believe what you want, but here's the message I came to deliver to you from the Attorney General and the President - leak one syllable to discredit Galahad and you will be arrested and tried for treason immediately and die in jail." Sullivan stood up, finished his drink, and walked toward the door. "I told you we couldn't trust Stein, he was never one of us. It's over."

21

The old man walked slowly from the library to the ultra modern office, which was located just off his bedroom between the kitchen and library. The house had been adapted for one floor living since the cancer began winning 14 months ago. He hated the fact that Sullivan would rather put his thing in a young man's behind instead of giving it to a young, fresh lass. He always thought it made him addleheaded, now he knew he was right. 'At the first real problem he resigns, he should have told #1 to shove it,' the old man said to himself. He tried to remember the last time he could keep an erection hard enough to ejaculate. The young ladies he hired over the years toyed and played with his flaccid manhood, but it had to be 15 or 20 years since he experienced the triumph of old faithful. One of Buehler's aides helped him into bed. "No dope until I'm done work," he ordered. The aide swung around a wall-mounted serving tray with a lap top computer and telephone on it. "Now leave, I have work to do." Buehler had to concentrate to fight off the fatigue the pain brought. He picked up the phone and made the first of several calls to his connections in the media. He ordered the discrediting of Galahad to be accelerated and begin immediately.

"We cannot do it now, sir," each of the news agencies reported back to the power broker.

"Why the fuck not! We've paid you well!" Buehler screamed. His outburst brought the aide back into his room and she started a morphine drip in his catheter. Buehler gave no objections.

"The White House released Brown's bio, 'he is a former Congressional Medal of Honor winning Green Beret who was put in the witness protection program after serving a successful career as an intelligence officer for the United States Government,'" the television executive quoted. "Hell, they even have an old picture of him from when he was in the army."

"So what, just run what I told you," Buehler ordered again.

"We cannot do that under these circumstances, sir. We would be wide open for libel and there's a buzz in the air that the White House would not look too kindly on that." All four news agencies the Alliance had arranged to begin snowballing Galahad's character had pulled out. Buehler moved on to the next order of business and called his military contacts.

"Get me in touch with former Vice President, Day," he ordered.

"Sir, it's 3:00 a.m., can't it wait until morning? Day is on a field trip, we must wait until he returns before we can get a message to him."

"Fuck you!" Buehler yelled, and disconnected the line. He looked up to see Sullivan's picture on the muted television set and gathered it was the announcement of his resignation. The morphine was beginning to take effect and the old power broker made one last call to the ranch in Austin.

"Hello?" a sleepy voice answered.

"It's me," Buehler said.

"Who's me?" the voice asked.

"King Arthur," Buehler answered.

"Who did you say you were?"

"It's me, Charles Buehler. Code word damage control, you idiot! You understand?"

"Oh, yeah, right. King Arthur, damage control. Partial or full?"

"Full, you idiot, swear it," Buehler ordered.

"Consider it done, your majesty," the voice replied. The phone went dead. The sun was rising and Buehler ordered his aide to turn his bed to the east and bring him some orange juice. 'The deep orange comes first,' he said, 'then it lightens, until it's yellow.' Before Buehler saw the yellow of the sunrise he broke the capsule he threatened Galahad with between his teeth. 'I win.'

Roger awoke from a light sleep early Thursday morning. He quietly climbed out of bed, pulled on a pair of jeans with a belt buckle of a bucking bronco, and donned his cowboy boots and a light weight flannel shirt. 'When in Rome,' he said softly, as he descended the stairs to put a pot of coffee on. The dawn was misty and overcast and it was hard to tell if the sun was actually coming up. He flipped on the radio and the news station confirmed a dreary day. Stein kept popping in his head and Roger knew the recurring in his thought was a signal, but for what? He was retrieving a mug out of the cabinet when he heard a light tapping on the kitchen door. To his surprise, it was the Green Beret hired hand.

"Sorry to disturb you colonel," the ex-soldier said.

"Come in, I have some coffee on." Roger did not like to sit around and shoot the bull with people who worked for him, or soldiers under his command, but under the circumstances he felt somewhat isolated. Although Cat tried to be supportive, he knew the predicament was a result of his actions, and it was his responsibility to clean it up. The soldier sat on one of the stools at the island and Roger grabbed another mug. As he poured the coffee the Green Beret said,

"May I be direct, sir?"

"Sure," Roger replied.

"I've been awake since 03:29 hours waiting for the lights to come on in the main house," the ex-Beret stated. The soldier's reference to military time awakened Roger's instincts; this was a debriefing, not an ordinary conversation. "Well, the old geezer had a little too much tequila last night and more passed out than went to sleep."

"Go on," Roger ordered.

"The phone rang at 03:29 hours, I noted the time on the digital alarm clock. The person on the line identified himself as King Arthur and kept babbling, 'code word damage control.' I was confused by the conversation, which seemed to irritate the man, and he further identified himself as Charles Bouder, or

Belder, or something." Roger almost spit out his coffee when he heard the story. Wiping his chin with a napkin he asked,

"Was his name Charles Buehler?"

"Yes, that's it, Buehler," the soldier said, enthusiastically. Roger sat quietly in thought for a few minutes.

"The old man never got the command, correct?"

"No, sir. I left the phone off the hook when I came over here," the ex-Beret replied.

"Good. Very good," Roger said.

"Does this mean what I think it means, sir?" the soldier asked.

"That the old man is not who he said he is? Absolutely," Roger stated. "He was their key contact for the details of our personal habits."

"Give me an order, sir," the Green Beret asked. At that moment the phone rang, startling both men. Roger answered it on the beginning of the second ring.

"Hello?"

"Stein here."

"How goes things?" Roger asked, walking away from the soldier.

"I'll be in Austin later today. You will surrender yourself tomorrow morning at 10:00 a.m. at the Austin court house for the charges of manslaughter and reckless endangerment. There will be a lot of favorable press thrown your way in the next few days and I expect payment as we agreed," Stein said.

"The remaining two parts of the conversation will be given to you tomorrow, you'll receive the last detail at the conclusion of the trial. No arguments, that's how it's going to be." Stein was silent for a moment.

"Fine, I'll see you tomorrow. Keep a low profile."

"One last thing," Roger said.

"What?"

"Use your connections to trace a call that was made to the hired hand's quarters about 3:30 a.m. this morning."

"Is it important?" Stein asked.

"Yes, and fax me your findings," Roger ordered, as he hung up the phone. He returned to the kitchen and offered the Beret a second cup of coffee. The phone rang again as he replaced the carafe.

"Hello?" Roger said, knowing it would be Stein.

"Watch the news, some very important announcements coming your way at 8:00 a.m. eastern," Stein said.

"Fine," Roger replied, "And my other request?"

"Check your fax machine. The call in question came from an unlisted number in Chevy Chase, Maryland. Watch the news." Stein hung up. Roger went to his office and found a single page on the fax machine. He returned to the kitchen and set the fax in front of the ex-Green Beret.

"You know the first order, make it look like an accident. Then I want you to check your quarters, all the barns and the main house for explosives and weapons," Roger ordered.

"Consider it done, sir," the soldier said, as he exited the house. Roger turned off the radio and flipped on the television set hanging above the breakfast bar. He sat at the counter and drank his coffee, trying to suppress the urge to go kill the old man with his bare hands. Cat limped into the kitchen and greeted him with a good morning kiss.

"You're up early," she said.

"You doing alright?" Roger asked.

"Just a little stiff, it's the weather," Cat replied. "What are you doing. . ." Roger cut her off,

"Hush."

"Roger brown, the millionaire rancher who single-handedly rescued his daughter from a group of terrorist kidnapers earlier this week, will be charged by the Justice Department tomorrow for reckless endangerment and manslaughter. For more on this story we go to our legal analyst, Mort Chin."

"There's more to this story than meets the eye. Roger Brown will be exemplified by the Justice Department, so people in this country see that no matter what the circumstances, vigilantism is against the law. We expect a national outcry on Mr. Brown's behalf. White House sources indicate Brown is actually Colonel Joseph Wilson, a former Green Beret and three-time Congressional Medal of Honor recipient, who, after serving over 15 years in the intelligence community, was given a new identity for reasons of national security. Sources also state the former Mr. Wilson retired from the intelligence community on good terms with the government. I questioned if Mr. Brown's service to his country would be taken into consideration, and the United States District Attorney's Office indicated Mr. Brown would be treated impartially, like any other United States citizen charged with the commission of a criminal offense. The National Security Administration has made it clear that Mr. Brown's involvement as an intelligence agent is classified information and no further details will be released."

"Thank you, Mort. Later today we'll take an inside look at Roger Brown, one of Austin's leading citizens. In other news, the White House released a statement early this morning the Chief of Staff, Thomas Sullivan has resigned due to health problems. Assistant Chief of Staff, Ellis Grady will temporarily assume his responsibilities. We'll be right back after this message."

"What do you make of that, honey?" Cat asked.

"Good. Very, very, very good," Roger said, leaning over to give his wife a kiss. Their eyes went back to the television as the news continued.

"A sad day in Washington, D.C. today, former United States Ambassador, Charles Buehler, was found dead at his estate early this morning. Buehler had been battling cancer since early last year. He will be remembered as a friend of democrats and republicans, and for his philanthropic donations for homeless children."

Roger turned to Cat, "Now that really made my day."

Working between two offices, Grady was up to his ears in administration problems. Everyone was his new best friend, trying to get on his good side and have his cause heard by the President. During his first morning as Acting Chief of Staff, #1 offered him some advice,

"Don't let the bastards get you down. You just make sure that the inner workings of the White House run in a professional, ethical manner, unlike your predecessor."

"Yes, sir," Grady answered, before briefing the President on his agenda for the day. "Do you want to release a statement about Charles Buehler's' death?"

"Of course," #1 said, "the usual condolences, and send the Vice President to the service. Anything else? I'd really like to have a three day weekend and take tomorrow off to play a little golf."

"Only that I received a fax from Israeli Ambassador, Glickman about the Austin situation, 'All fine. Other two conversations will be collected at the court house. Mona Lisa at conclusion of trial.'" Grady read.

"That makes sense," #1 said, after a moment of thought. "Galahad gives up the other two tapes of his conversation with Buehler now, and the disc when the trial is over. Hell, it's exactly what I would do if I were him."

"Can we trust him to give the disc back when the trial is over?" Grady asked.

"Yes. You keep him popular in the media's eye, the Attorney General, assured me of a quick trial. When it's over, I believe Galahad will give us the disc and then he and his family will disappear forever. He did not break the agreement, the Alliance and the government did, through Sullivan and Day. Just keep an eye on things in Austin, I have a feeling everything is to turn out okay."

Roger was helping the housekeeper prepare a rainy day lunch of soup and sandwiches while Cat and Tris played in the basement. The voice of the ex-Green Beret could be heard in the distance, growing louder as he approached the main house from the barn.

"Colonel, colonel," the soldier yelled, through the rain. Roger opened the back door to see what all the commotion was about. "Colonel, there's been an accident, the old man is hurt bad," the soldier said.

"Where?" Roger asked.

"On the other side of the barn." Roger turned to the housekeeper,

"Call an ambulance," he ordered. Twenty-five minutes later the paramedics loaded his lifeless body into the ambulance. The sheriff did a routine investigation, questioning Roger and grilling the Green Beret-hired hand. The ex-soldier gave his account of the old man climbing up on the roof to close the vent to protect the hay from the heavy rain. His story was backed up by one set of muddy footprints on the roof. The coroner's office later confirmed his death was due to a broken neck, but noted his blood alcohol level was twice the legal limit. The Austin police, figuring the Brown's had been through enough, called the old man's death an accident and closed the case. After the police left, the Beret led Roger to one of the other barns. Atop one of the rafters was a 30.06 rifle, two .38 caliber handguns and enough C-4 explosive to bring down the main house and then some.

"Keep searching, make sure there are no charges set; and do your best at feeding the cattle," Roger ordered.

"Yes, sir," the soldier replied. Roger turned as he headed for the house,

"You did very well."

22

Roger was chauffeured to the Austin courthouse by the ex-Green Beret. Cat and Tris remained at the ranch with the housekeeper, awaiting Dr. Francis. As Roger's car exited the gates of the ranch, four television news vans followed him. Roger was relieved that the media obeyed the no trespassing signs posted on the edge of the property. When he opened the car door in front of the court house, the news cameras began rolling, reporters stuck microphones in his face, and a thousand pictures were snapped. The police cleared a path for Roger to climb the stairs to the courthouse. It was a bright, sunny day, not as hot as it was earlier in the week, but a day when the sun could play tricks on your eyes. Inside the dark courthouse Roger heard a familiar voice,

"Mr. Brown, you are under arrest for manslaughter and reckless endangerment."

"This is a sick joke, Taylor," Roger said, as the FBI Agent handcuffed him and read him his rights. Roger was processed, mug shots and all, and put in a holding cell. The paperwork and photo session took about ninety minutes and Roger spent another hour in the urine stained 8 x 10 cell before Stein arrived. A guard unlocked the cell and re-cuffed Roger while Stein waited outside.

"What's going on, Stein?" Roger asked, firmly.

"Calm down, everything's under control," Stein replied.

"It better be," Roger said, making eye contact with the Philadelphia lawyer.

The Honorable William Joseph Cowen was the sitting judge at the arraignment.

"Case #14012-A, the State of Texas and the United States Government versus Roger Brown, also known as Joseph Wilson." Stein arranged for a closed court due to the media coverage and only a dozen people were present in the courtroom. "Mr. Brown you are charged with manslaughter and reckless endangerment. How do you plead?" The Honorable Billy Joe Cowen asked.

"Your Honor, may I request a moment in chambers with you, opposing counsel, FBI Agent, Taylor and my client?" Stein asked.

"This is only an arraignment counselor, I don't know how they practice law where you're from, but here, my job is only to decide if there is enough evidence to order a trial," Judge Cowen replied.

"Your Honor, I am in possession of some information that may expedite these proceedings. Due to the sensitive nature of the information I feel it is best to discuss it in the privacy of your chambers. I assure you it is pertinent to your decision," Stein said.

"Mr. Prosecutors, what do you think?" Judge Cowen asked. There were two attorneys presenting opposing counsel, one from the State of Texas and one from the United States Attorney General's Office. The Federal D.A., who was acting as lead counsel, knew he had drawn the shittiest case of the decade and thought he may be able to save a little face.

"No objections, your Honor."

"Fine, let's take this party to my chambers." All concerned parties followed the bailiff to the Judges anteroom, which was too small to hold everyone comfortably. Only Stein and the lead counsel for the prosecution had chairs. The bailiff was dismissed due to lack of space, but handcuffed Roger before leaving the room.

"If I may, your Honor, I wanted to bring to the court's attention that all charges against my client are true," Stein opened.

"That's a hell of a defense, counselor," the Judge replied.

"Your Honor, we are not here to waste the court's time, or the taxpayers money, on a long, drawn out trial that will attract more media attention than the O.J. Simpson case," Stein stated.

"Then you are going to plead guilty?" Judge Cowen asked.

"No, your Honor, not quite. I am here to inform the court that Mr. Brown was working on behalf, or should I say with the knowledge of, the proper authorities," Stein said.

"What are you saying counselor, that the United States Government knew your client was going to kill the kidnappers?" the judge asked, with the volume of his voice increasing.

"In a word, yes. Agent Taylor will testify that his Station Chief, Anthony Bucco, had instructed the FBI to let Mr. Brown handle the case and divert the investigation in another direction," Stein said.

"Why in God's name would the FBI do that?" Judge Cowen asked, directing his question to Taylor.

"Your Honor, it was decided at the highest level, with the recommendation of the Bureau, that Mr. Brown was the most qualified person to attempt to secure the return of his daughter. Although the deaths of the kidnapers were unfortunate, the United States Government does not negotiate with terrorists," Taylor answered.

"How high of a level, Agent Taylor?" the judge asked. Taylor presented a letter drafted by the Acting Chief of Staff to the President of the United States, to the judge. The epistle evinced the reasons the United States Government authorized Brown's appointment to the Austin kidnaping case. Judge Cowen donned his reading glasses and examined the letter.

"So, in reality Brown was acting as a commissioned member of law enforcement," the Judge stated.

"Yes, your Honor," Stein confirmed.

"Counselor, what do you have to say?" the judge asked the federal prosecutor.

"I'm completely in the dark here, your Honor, but I was briefed that this would be a peculiar trial," the young D.A. said.

"Who briefed you?" the judge asked.

"The Attorney General himself. Agent Taylor is correct, the United States Government does not negotiate with terrorists; so, in a sense, Mr. Brown's actions were justified."

"So, what do you want me to do?" the judge asked.

"Throw the case out on the technicality that Mr. Brown was acting as a law enforcement agent," Stein said. The judge shook his head in silence for a moment, and then directed his commentary to Roger,

"If this ever happens again, give me a call and I'll help you track the bastards down." Roger smiled. He was released forty-five minutes later after a White House press statement elucidated that Roger Brown was acting on behalf of the FBI, and all formal charges were dropped at their request. The White House also reminded viewers that vigilantism is illegal, and the Attorney General will prosecute anyone who takes the law into his own hands to the fullest extent.

Stein stopped Roger on the way out of the court room.

"I believe you owe me something." Roger retrieved the two microcassettes from his jacket pocket and gave them to Stein. "And the disc?" Stein asked, calmly.

"Why Irving, you already have it. Look under that 19th century oak desk in your office," Roger said.

The ex-Green Beret drove Roger home, where messages from Barbara Walters to Larry King begged for interviews. Roger asked the housekeeper to call each one back and politely decline. It had done Roger's heart good to hear the former Chief of Staff, Thomas Sullivan died of a heart attack the same day he was arraigned at the court house in Austin. It also pleased him to learn former Vice President Day was diagnosed with Alzheimer's disease earlier that week and admitted to a hospice facility. Roger pushed hard to have the ranch sold, he knew his family could not stay there and live a normal life. Tris would always be the little girl who was kidnaped, Cat, the mother who was shot trying to save her child, and Roger, the father who killed five terrorists while working for the FBI. It was time to leave Austin.

Roger retreated to the sanctuary of the lower basement and made several phone calls to his Swiss banker. He re-routed the monies from one account in Switzerland, to an account in the Cayman Islands, and then back to another Swiss bank. He repeated the process until the original account Stein set up was depleted. The new Swiss account only held half the money, the other half was invisibly deposited in Peter Bishop's account in New Zealand. Roger had a trust set up for his housekeeper, who had been with them for five years, and then pulled the Green Beret aside and informed him that he wanted to make sure he was rewarded for his undying loyalty.

"Danny." Roger called the soldier by his given name, Daniel McBride.

"Yes, sir," Danny answered.

"Do you understand me?" Roger asked, again.

"Yes, sir, you put a little aside for me. It's appreciated, but it's not necessary." Danny replied.

"Listen, this is an order. If you don't have contact with me every week, you take your passport and fly to Switzerland," Roger said, as he handed McBride his passport. "The First Bank of Austin has $500,000 in your name, take some cash and buy a first class ticket to Switzerland, there will be further instructions waiting for you at the Zurich post office. This is very important for your health and welfare," Roger said.

"Yes, sir, consider it done. If I don't have any contact with you in a week, I'll take some cash, buy a ticket with the money at First Austin, and await further orders at the post office in Zurich," McBride repeated, not understanding why, but knowing his duty was to do and die.

Roger did not go into detail with Cathy about the when's and how's, but she kept a bag of their most precious belongings on notice. Roger sold the remaining cattle and signed over power of attorney to the First Bank of Austin to complete the sale of the ranch.

"Well, Mr. Brown, after all transactions are finalized, you're going to have close to $900 million invested with us," the excited banker told Roger, as figures from fees paid to the bank danced in his head.

"Fine. Put everything into the trust, pay the required taxes, and I'll let you know what I want done from there after I return from my around the world vacation," Roger stated. His final stop was the Austin attorney's office where Roger provided his lawyer with a codicil to their last will and testament.

The Brown's left on their around the world vacation the June following the kidnaping. The first stop was at DisneyWorld in Orlando, then down to Miami, stopping along the way to see the south Florida sights. From there they boarded a 747 bound for London, England and spent a few days in the United Kingdom before seeing Paris, Rome, and Athens. The Brown's were having the time of their life while slowly transforming into the Bishops. Six weeks later they arrived in Tokyo. All three of the Bishop's cleared Japanese immigration with their passports. After two weeks of sightseeing in the Far East, the Bishop's transformed from the Brown's of the United states to the Bishop's of New Zealand. Peter, Jennifer and Ellen Bishop moved into their new estate on ten acres in the New Zealand countryside. The complete identity transfer took four months, three days, and $91 million.

23

The kidnaping was a year and a half ancient history and the Bishop's were well adjusted to their new identities and surroundings in New Zealand. Cathy had reconstructive plastic surgery on her right cheek and right breast in Sydney, and no longer had to worry about her husband becoming an ass man. Tris attended a private school near East Cap, a twenty minute ride from their estate, and was beginning to lose her Texas accent. Roger and Cat told her it was a tradition in New Zealand to use a woman's maiden name and, out of respect for her grandmother, her given name would be changed from Tris to Ellen. The fact that she was five made the white lies a little easier. They had a small hen house with a few dozen chickens, a barn with three horses, and two Golden Retrievers. The Brown's found solace with their new identities and location.

Roger kept reflecting on the kidnaping, and his instincts still told him Stein was involved. He was not going to feel his family was completely safe until he rectified his suspicions. On a beautiful, hot February day, Roger told Cat he was returning to Austin to finalize the paperwork for the sale of the ranch, and he expected the business to take him about a week. He made two reservations back to Austin, one as Peter Bishop and one as Thomas Gallagher. Roger arrived in Honolulu as Peter Bishop and cleared United States Customs. His luggage went on to Austin, while he purchased a ticket to Philadelphia via Chicago as Thomas Gallagher. He arrived in Philadelphia at 7:42 p.m. on Thursday evening, rented a car at the airport, and drove to Stein's estate in Wynnewood, the Jewish section of the Main

Line. Stein's security system was augmented by four Doberman Pincers, who became Roger's good friends after his gift of fresh ground sirloin. He strolled onto the grounds, without so much as a bark, disabled the alarm system, and slipped into the ancient house. He noticed the decor was much the same as Stein's office at One Logan Square. He navigated the hallways and stairs in the darkness and found Stein, in what he surmised was the master bedroom, engaged in sex with a woman about his age. Stein was not a handsome man, but the woman, who turned out to be his housekeeper, gave Peggy Short a run for her money. The sight of the two of them having sex was almost immoral.

"Stein," Roger bellowed in a loud, booming voice, as he flipped on the light. His eyes adjusted to the brightness while the twosome flailed for the sheets.

"Who's there?" Stein yelled, reaching for his glasses. "My God, you scared me half to death," Stein screeched.

"Can you ask your wife to leave us?" Roger asked, in a level, businesslike tone.

"She's not my wife, I. . ." Stein's words trailed off.

"Then perhaps the lady can prepare some coffee for us," Roger said, as he walked to the edge of the hand-made bed. Stein ordered the woman to make a pot of coffee and prepare a snack for their guest. She ran from the bed to the adjoining bathroom, her copious flesh bouncing behind her, and slipped downstairs a few minutes later in a white uniform.

"What right do you have breaking into my house!" Stein demanded, as he reached for his robe. Roger wondered why skinny men liked fat women.

"I think we have some unfinished business."

"What do you mean? You have your daughter back and your anonymity," Stein countered.

"And my Swiss account, what happened to that?" Roger asked.

"I don't know. Half the money disappeared, but I was never able to trace it," Stein pleaded, assuming he now knew why Brown was there.

"Why did you check the account in the first place?" Roger asked.

"What do you mean?"

"Why would you check the account after the trial? You had no connection to it anymore," Roger said, as he sat in a chair by the window.

"I was curious to see where you were," Stein said, fumbling for words.

"Uh, huh. You have two choices, one is to die the worst death you can imagine, the other is to tell me the truth and die quickly," Roger said, offering Stein the same choice he offered the female kidnapper, Illiana.

"I swear I don't know what you're talking about," Stein answered. Roger leapt from the chair, grabbed Stein's left arm, and twisted it behind his back, breaking it at the elbow. Stein cried out in pain. He continued to deny any knowledge regarding Roger's inquires, and Roger continued to break more limbs. After having his scrotum slashed open to expose his testicles and being blinded in his right eye, Stein relented.

"Okay, stop, please stop!" Stein pleaded, as his tears diluted the stream of blood pouring from his eye. The maid appeared in the doorway and Roger asked her to put the tray of coffee and biscotti on the dresser. As she turned to leave, he shot her twice in the head.

"Now, what were you saying?" Roger asked.

"Buehler offered me some contracts for Israel if I could assist in relocating you," Stein said. Roger threw the pitcher of hot coffee on him and Stein screamed in agony, grabbing for the raw flesh that was once his balls.

"Go on," Roger ordered.

"Through the Swiss accounts I let him know you were dealing with the First Bank of Austin. He had a man working underground for him, but I believe you killed him," Stein said.

"The ranch hand?" Roger asked.

"Yes, I think," Stein said, feeling the agony of Christ on the cross.

"Why you?" Roger asked.

"Buehler learned I was the head of the Mesad and was blackmailing me, besides, the contracts were good business. I screwed up their plans when I had the Israeli Ambassador go to the White House after your visit to my office," Stein explained.

"How did Buehler know you were involved with the Mesad?" Roger asked.

"He put two and two together, the Mesad's operations in the Middle East, its high success ratio. . . . He traced the money back to the United States with the assistance of the Alliance. I figure they uncovered my true identity a little over two years ago," Stein winced, trying to stop the blood from his groin with his unbroken limb. "I made one mistake, I had Israel capitalize on the misfortune of the Arab's too quickly after the Gulf War. According to Buehler, this set the balance of power out of whack in the region." Stein reached for a cigarette and Roger lit it for him.

"Go on," Roger ordered.

"Buehler and the Alliance knew I was Galahad's connection to the world. . . ."

"So, they offered you a position in the Alliance?" Roger asked.

"They feared I might come into possession of the disc you stole and expose them," Stein offered. Roger half smiled,

"And if you were part of the Alliance, you would expose yourself as well. Why did you change sides?"

"Because Buehler was going after you for revenge. There was no reason to take you out of the deep freeze. I always dealt with you on a business level and conducted my career on a business level, Buehler crossed the line. There was no profit to be made, his motive was purely that of a dying man trying to even the score," Stein said.

"Then why did you keep me alive for five years after I retired?"

"It was a cover to scare people and keep the upper hand in our black ops, but Buehler saw through it after a few years. I honestly tried to help you when I realized it was personal between you and Buehler." Roger raised his gun and shot Stein three times in the head.

"Nothing personal," Roger said.

Thomas Gallagher left Philadelphia International Airport at 4:01 a.m. Four airports and 22 hours later, Peter Bishop arrived in Auckland, New Zealand.

About the Author

Born in 1956, I was raised in South Philadelphia and currently reside in Horsham, Pennsylvania, a northern suburb of the city. I retired from a career as a financial consultant with a large U.S. insurance company in 1996. I graduated the American College in Bryn Mawr, Pennsylvania and hold the professional designations CLU and ChFC. I am married with one child and a playful Maltese named "Chablis." I stumbled upon writing as a hobby to pass the time in my retirement. In addition to expressing my imagination on paper, I enjoy golf, travel, wine collecting and baseball.